9 781576 730713

DIARY OF GOD

Diary of God

Diary of God

Stories of God's incredible encounters with his people

Ron Rose

DIARY OF GOD
published by Multnomah Publishers, Inc.

© 1997 by Ron Rose

International Standard Book Number: 1-57673-071-9
Printed in the United States of America

Unless otherwise noted, scriptures are quoted from *The Holy Bible, New Century Version* (NCV)
copyright © 1987, 1988, 1991 by Word Publishing, Dallas, Texas 75234. Used by permission.

Also quoted:
The Holy Bible, New International Version (NIV) © 1973, 1984 by International Bible Society,
used by permission of Zondervan Publishing House

The Message, © 1993 by Eugene H. Peterson

For information:
MULTNOMAH PUBLISHERS, INC.
POST OFFICE BOX 1720
SISTERS, OREGON 97759

Library of Congress Cataloging-in-Publication Data:
Rose, Ron.
    Diary of God/by Ron Rose.
        p.cm.   Includes index.   ISBN 1-57673-071-9 (alk. paper)
    1. Bible--Devotional literature.   I. Title
    BS491.5.R67   1997   97-19706
    242'.5--dc21   CIP

97 98 99 00 01 02 03 04 – 10 9 8 7 6 5 4 3 2 1

Contents

LORD my God, you are very great.
You are clothed with glory and majesty;
    you wear light like a robe.
You stretch out the skies like a tent.
    You build your room above the clouds.
You make the clouds your chariot,
    and you ride on the wings of the wind.
You make the winds your messengers,
    and flames of fire are your servants.

You built the earth on its foundations
    so it can never be moved.
You covered the earth with oceans;
    the water was above the mountains.
But at your command, the water rushed away.
    When you thundered your orders, it hurried away.
The mountains rose; the valleys sank.
    The water went to the places you made for it.
You set borders for the seas that they cannot cross,
    so water will never cover the earth again.

You make springs pour into the ravines;
    they flow between the mountains....
You water the mountains from above.
    The earth is full of the things you made.

PSALM 104:1–13

Introduction

I will make them want to know me, that I am the LORD. They
will be my people, and I will be their God, because they will
return to me with their whole hearts. (Jeremiah 24:7)

For a long time I was convinced it was impossible to really know the God of the universe. After all, he's more powerful, more just, more righteous, more intriguing, more holy, more forgiving, more tenacious, more majestic, and more surprising than we can begin to comprehend. Our language doesn't have the words to capture his greatness; he is totally and emphatically beyond us and our imaginations. Yet, we yearn to know him.

The almighty God wills for his people to get to know him without reserve. The God who exists in a spiritual world beyond our five senses has invaded our world with an invitation for relationship in hand. Since the beginning, he has found ways to encounter his people. Marvel of marvels, he planned it from the beginning—and made it so! God, the master of the impossible, wants us to know him face to face, and he provides the way. Our limited words, puny understandings, and cramped imaginations won't stop him.

God's lavish plans for us have unfolded over generations on this earth, while we are limited to our meager seventy-year perspective. The boundless, timeless, peerless God of creation—the God who puts color in the world and sound in the air—has already planned a one-on-one, personal relationship with us. He wants us to know him as an involved, committed, protective, and ever-present Father God. As his children, he loves us, not because of who we are, but because of who he is. Even when we are the most unlovable, he loves us. We can't stop him from loving us; we can't move far enough, dawdle long enough, or protest loud enough to stop him.

He planned for the times his children would try to live without him and for the times they would return to him.

INVADING MY WORLD

I was comfortable studying *about* God, without thinking at all about actually knowing him. I had studied theology; I knew all the "-ation" words like *justification, sanctification,* and *reconciliation.* I stood for the Truth, served on church committees, attended all the potlucks, and studied the Bible regularly. I had all my church "ducks" in a row, so to speak. I knew a lot about God, but I'd not yet met him. I knew the book but had never met the author.

When my life slowed down long enough for me to think, I found a disturbing lack of peace, a spiritual restlessness that alarmed me. Assuming I was suffering from one of those yet-to-be-identified, environment-related syndromes, I stubbornly ignored the uneasiness, thinking it would go away. It was a "man thing"—don't think about it or talk about it, and it will go away. There were plenty of things to distract me, and as long as I stayed busy, I was fine. I packed my schedule full of amusements and did whatever it took to avoid periods of silence.

Then in the unbearable quiet of a sleepless night, God reached inside and touched my soul. His invisible presence invaded my world. I couldn't explain it, nor did I understand it. Somehow my distinct, detached, and distant God overwhelmed my senses. The invitation was undeniable. I encountered the presence of the God of creation, and he knew my name. In spite of my busyness, my stubbornness, and my denial, God found a way to break through to my soul, whether I liked it or not.

OPENING THE EYES OF YOUR HEART

For as long as this planet has been populated, God has found ways to encounter his people. The Bible is the epic record of his incredible encounters with his people. This holy book was never meant to be merely a textbook or a proof text. It's more like a diary, filled with stories and insights about God and his people. Within its pages, God reveals himself in the lives of ordinary people. But it's not a private diary, locked up and hidden away in a secret place. It's available and familiar. He wants us to open it, to read it, and to get to know him.

What a tragedy it would be to spend a lifetime bumping into God, brushing up against him, but never making face-to-face contact—never getting to know the person behind the name. Possessing a head full of facts about God doesn't mean we know him or that we're close to him. We can quote him in any version from the King James to The Living Bible without knowing the God who gave the quote. We can study his Word like a rule book and become careful rule keepers without even expecting to know the rule giver. We can even retell the glorious biblical story and stand at a distance, unaffected and uninvolved. We can even rely on his promises and worship him weekly and still not know him.

But God's encounters always invade the soul. They lift our spirits, open our eyes, transform our hearts, and claim our allegiance. God seems to enjoy shattering our limited understanding of him. Just when we think we have him figured out, just when he begins to fit within the borders of our imagination, he expands the borders. Nothing we can dream up will ever confine him. Getting to know the giver of life is an eternal project. There will always be more to know—more truths to hear, more experiences to share, more wisdom to learn, and more mysteries to probe.

AN INTRODUCTION'S IN ORDER

The Diary of God recounts only a few of the stories of God's incredible encounters with his people recorded in his Word. Each story reveals a God intimately involved in life on this earth. Combined, they chronicle God's desire to personally connect with ordinary, struggling, stubborn, self-reliant people like you and me. You may recognize the stories, the people, and the places, but my prayer is that you may hear, as I have, God inviting you to a relationship, a closer, more personal relationship than ever before.

God took the first step in this relationship before the clocks were wound, before order conquered chaos, before Eden had sod—and he hasn't stopped. Our God still...

initiates,
promises,
rescues,
comforts,
forgives,
heals,
confronts,
encourages,
corrects,
protects,
surprises,
provides,
defends,
allures,
rejoices,
and, most of all, invites.

He invites us into relationship with him.

In this diary we join our ancestors in the quest to know our creator—the ever-present God who already knows us. We focus not on facts but on holy moments and experiences to be shared—on God's encounters with us.

Your place in the diary is still being written. As he did with the generations before us, God calls us to be his people and then fills our lives with spiritual power to see beyond ourselves, drawing us close to him. And like those who have come before us, we will find spiritual intimacy with our

Creator God in both the most familiar and unexpected places.

Begin with me in the imagination of God and prepare for a divine encounter. God already knows your name, your secrets, your frustrations, your strengths, your hopes, your dreams.

Now he wants you to come to know him.

The creation receives a soul

A long time ago in the uncharted regions of heaven, God imagined a world of light and love, a world of peace and security, a world without fear or frustration or rejection. It would be the perfect setting for the people he had in mind—people made in his image. These people would become the unique beneficiaries of his unending love.

Then, God spoke the words and made it so. Out of a shapeless void, he created a perfect world. But the finale of his creative masterpiece was mankind. He took dirt from the new ground and transformed it into the first human being. In all the universe only this creature was made in the image of the creator. With God's own breath, the creature became a living, divine original—personally autographed by the Creator God.

God's new person was more than a biological marvel. Mankind was designed to reason independent of instinct, to dream and sing and express emotion, to create and build and invent, to feel love and compassion and hope, to ask why and why not. Hidden deep within was an unnamed restlessness, a yearning for God, a spiritual legacy—the unique part of mankind that carries in it the presence of God. In the best way possible the creature took after the creator. A touch of the divine made God's creation more than flesh and blood, more than life. The creature received an eternal soul.

Everything was in its place. The greatest saga of love had begun, and God, the author of it all, was pleased.

Reflection: Every person God makes is still a divine original with a divine legacy—a soul. The soul is our birthday gift from the creator, the home of our spiritual essence, the source of our yearning for life beyond ourselves. Although the soul cannot be humanly explained or adequately described, it is, at the deepest level, everything we are. And our souls are just as eager to live in constant relationship with the creator as was the soul of the first human.

So God created human beings in his image. In the image of God he created them.

GENESIS 1:27

God creates the human family

God helped his new creation realize what God himself already knew—it isn't good to be alone. He put the original to sleep and shaped from the first human a companion, a wife. When Adam woke up, he must have been amazed. Unlike every other creature in his paradise, she was like him, and yet not just like him. Alike, yet different. Part of him, yet distinct. Another divine mystery.

God's divine original had become two—man and woman. They would spend the rest of their lives experiencing and treasuring moments of oneness. The delighted Creator God had given them to each other for togetherness, for life. The gift of marriage was unwrapped that day.

Adam and Eve lived in and cared for God's private garden. Each day they learned more about each other and the mysterious, all-powerful, but gentle being who had filled their bodies with life, their heads with wonder, their hearts with feelings, and their spirits with purity.

In this world called Eden, God was their future, their heritage, and their daily guide. They lived without concern for personal needs or a sense of danger; God provided everything. They had everything to learn, but their Creator God was an excellent tutor, and they had all the time in the world. God must have been thrilled; his dream had been realized.

Reflection: In Eden there were no masks to take off, no fears to overcome, and no past failures to live down. Closeness with God wasn't second nature—it was first nature. And human closeness inherited its pattern from closeness with God himself.

Today, in our struggle to build lasting marriages and our search for the secrets of oneness, we have turned our attention to intimacy and happiness and have undermined the original purpose of marriage: to serve together in the presence of God—lifting each other closer to him, working together for his purposes, his tasks, his calling. When we do that, God gives us what we need. After all, God is the inventor of human relationships. He knows what his creation needs.

Then the LORD God said, "It is not good for the man to be alone. I will make a helper who is right for him."

From the ground God formed every wild animal and every bird in the sky, and he brought them to the man so the man could name them. Whatever the man called each living thing, that became its name. The man gave names to all the tame animals, to the birds in the sky, and to all the wild animals. But Adam did not find a helper that was right for him.

GENESIS 2:18–20

Facing consequences

Everything was going so well when scandalous news rocked the depths of the Garden and the gates of heaven. Angels were stunned. God was heartbroken. The dream appeared hopelessly shattered.

Adam and Eve had disobeyed God's commands and had lost their innocence. Thinking they could be like God, they ate the forbidden fruit that would give them instant wisdom and the need for a conscience. Life on earth would never be the same, for any sin, any disobedience of God, separates us from the perfection of heaven. God's beloved couple was now sentenced to acquire their own knowledge, make their own living, create their own world, and feel their pain, outside of God's protective Garden.

In this single act Adam and Eve brought death and decay into the world and gave Satan a foothold in God's creation. Fear and failure were added to the tapestry of life; conflict and frustration soon followed. The consequences of Adam and Eve's unfaithfulness forced them from the Garden and from the presence of God, but not from his love. In a parting act of compassion God made clothes for his now dying creation.

Reflection: It's impossible for us to grasp the pain Adam and Eve must have felt the day they walked out of the Garden. The consequence of their sin was clear—death, and the fear and dread it brings. But it would be centuries before they physically paid that price. On eviction day, they also gave up what we long for, a peace of mind and contentment found only in the presence of God. Their sin introduced the world to broken relationships and alienation, a condition worse than physical death.

But God already had his plan for redemption in place—a no-expense-spared, secret plan to rescue his unfaithful people and restore his relationship with them forever. This is a God with a plan bigger than our mistakes.

Sin came into the world because of what one man did, and with sin came death. This is why everyone must die—because everyone sinned.

ROMANS 5:12

Experiencing the pain of death

For Adam and Eve, life outside the Garden was filled with struggle, disappointment, and uncertainty. Work was hard. There were no relatives for support, no neighbors to engage in backyard conversations, no parents to tell stories of the way things used to be. While sensing an emptiness in their souls, Adam and Eve must have learned many lessons through painful trial and error.

Adam and Eve's sin had given death an entrée into the world. While their own deaths were still centuries away, it invaded their home—their firstborn son, Cain, murdered his younger brother, Abel. The double grief of losing Abel to death and Cain to the discipline of God left Adam and Eve alone and facing the reality of death. The memory of their Garden time with God must have made the pain of death and the separation even worse.

As God's first family dealt with life and death separated from his presence, and new children replaced Cain and Abel, people began the practice of prayer.

Reflection: It seems natural that people began praying after they experienced grief. Nothing causes us to rethink our priorities, our values, and our relationship with God like the death of a loved one. Death always reminds us of our own mortality and that we are not in control.

Death empties our hearts and calls us to prayer—not a "give me" prayer or a self-promoting prayer, but an intimate outpouring of tears and pain. No mere repetition of familiar words, no intellectual discussion with God, prayer at these times becomes an unguarded, heartfelt conversation with our listening God. And only through our conversations with him can we feel at home in his presence.

When people are tempted, they should not say, "God is tempting me." Evil cannot tempt God, and God himself does not tempt anyone. But people are tempted when their own evil desire leads them away and traps them. This desire leads to sin, and then the sin grows and brings death.

JAMES 1:13–15

The world starts over

After the death of Adam and Eve, life on earth grew more violent and evil. People lived over nine hundred years, but long life didn't mean they spent more time with God. They lived for themselves, acting as their own guides. Without shame, God's fallen people had transformed God's world into a faithless nightmare. Granted, he didn't create them to be puppets, controlled by every twitch of his fingers; he created them with freedom to choose their own direction. But once they discovered their own power, they walked away from the One who created them. And the almighty Creator God regretted his own creation. Imagine heaven draped with sadness — God allowing his heart to be filled with sorrow and pain.

But, there was hope.

Noah's family continued to walk with God outside the long lost Garden. Enoch, Noah's great-grandfather, had found a heart path to God and "walked" there constantly. Their relationship was so extraordinary that God had taken Enoch home, sparing him the experience of death. Noah surely knew that story well. He, too, was a good man who lived by God's compass despite the conditions in his world.

Hundreds of years had passed since Adam and Eve were created in the Garden. Now God decided to start over with humankind. God told Noah to build an ark — a big barge, a watertight hotel for animals, because it was about to rain and rain and rain. Although neither Noah nor anybody else had ever seen it rain, Noah obeyed. Surely Noah must have wondered, questioned — building something that had never been seen or needed or even imagined before. He understood later, but he began by faithfully trusting God and building the barge. Once completed and filled with Noah, his family, and representatives of all the animals, God released the underground springs and turned on the forty-day rain. Eventually water covered the whole earth, but those in the floating zoo were safe and dry.

Together, Noah's family and the chosen animals spent over a year in that big barge while the world beneath them was being washed clean. When they finally stepped out onto dry land, they thanked God for keeping his dream alive and for choosing them to be part of it.

Reflection: Don't you imagine there were evenings when a sleepless Noah lay there wondering what in the world he was doing, wishing he understood more about the why? At times God asks us to do things we've never done, go places we've never been, and experience things we've not even thought of. It's not his way to force us beyond our will; he never coerces our reply or our relationship. He chooses to be our guide, invites us to go beyond our comfort zones, deepens our confidence in him, and draws us closer to him. Our response shouldn't require understanding, but faith.

The LORD saw that the human beings on the earth were very wicked and that everything they thought about was evil. He was sorry he had made human beings on the earth, and his heart was filled with pain.... But Noah pleased the LORD.

GENESIS 6:5–8

It was by faith that Noah heard God's warnings about things he could not yet see. He obeyed God and built a large boat to save his family. By his faith, Noah showed that the world was wrong, and he became one of those who are made right with God through faith.

HEBREWS 11:7

Starting over with promise

After the flood, God put limits on himself and issued his first postcreation promise to earth's population. He vowed never again to destroy all life on earth with water, and the rainbow is a reminder of that promise. Without it, the descendants of Noah might have panicked at every afternoon thunderstorm. A relationship with God might have been based on dread and fear. The rainbow—seen as a full circle from the heavens and as a half-circle on earth—reminded God's new population that he is still in charge and that life is based on faith, not fear.

The reborn earth was fresh and clean, but it wasn't the Garden of Eden. Noah and his family still lived in a world shadowed by disobedience, loneliness, injustice, selfishness, and sin. As Noah's family reestablished humankind on earth, God blessed them and encouraged them to have lots of children, which they did. It was his plan to *lead* his people—his struggling, frightened, and forgetful people—from the ark to heaven, from the rainbow on earth to the rainbow surrounding his throne. In between God's rainbows of promise are the storms of life, and in the storms God's people find themselves standing on the promises.

Reflection: To build a lasting relationship with his creation, God is confronted with a strategic dilemma—his people must know enough about him to fear his awesome power, but fear of his power will suffocate their relationship with him.

God's response is perfect. He counters our human fearfulness with a public promise in the sky. The rainbow gently reminds him, and us, of his promise never to destroy the earth with water. He voluntarily places the sign of his promise where everyone can see it and remember the God behind it. Regardless of the clouds, we can look forward to our future with God with confidence.

Our journey to the heart of God must start with an awareness of his unmatched, awesome power and his unbending demands of virtue and holiness. Any other basis is dishonest and destructive. But our journey takes us beyond his power toward dependence on his promises. His promises open the door to relationship with him, and while defusing our fears, they nurture our hope.

What a mighty God we serve. He, the ultimate promise keeper, values his creation as if we were worthy of his promises.

When the rainbow appears in the clouds, I will see it and I will remember the agreement that continues forever between me and every living thing on the earth.

GENESIS 9:16

The birth of misunderstanding

As the years passed, Noah's descendants stayed in Babylon, growing more self-reliant and self-indulgent. There they established a strong city and banded together to make a name for themselves. Impressed by their own ingenuity and power, they began building a tower to the heavens as a monument to themselves.

God was displeased with their self-centered attempts at greatness, but he chose not to destroy the tower or to harm the people. Without warning he simply confused their speech; no longer could they understand each other's words. Not only did work on the tower stop, but the people no longer could live together in community. God scattered them over all the earth. The descendants of Ham migrated toward Africa, the descendants of Japheth headed westward toward Europe, and the clan of Shem stayed around the city of Ur in Babylon.

Reflection: When God introduced new languages at the tower of Babel, he made mankind forever vulnerable to communication difficulties and deficiencies. And without communication, misunderstanding is probable and community is impossible. Yet, our human failures to communicate point out the great blessing of our relationship with the Father of words. When we don't know the words to use, he understands anyway. We're limited by our words; he is not.

All the earth should worship
    the LORD;
    the whole world should fear
    him.
He spoke, and it happened.
    He commanded, and it appeared.
The LORD upsets the plans of
    nations;
    he ruins all their plans.
But the LORD's plans will stand
    forever;
    his ideas will last from now on....
The LORD looks down from heaven
    and sees every person.
From his throne he watches
    all who live on earth.
He made their hearts
    and understands everything
    they do.

PSALM 33:8–15

Looking for a friend

Centuries later the citizens of Ur had developed their community into a showplace. For its time, Ur was a thriving, advanced metropolitan area, civilized and comfortable. The people had running water in their homes, a code of laws, public schools, financial institutions, shops, and a social structure. They also had their own gods.

Abraham grew up in that community. But his comfortable days in the city were interrupted by an extraordinary invitation from God. God called Abraham to leave the security of home, the benefits of city life, and the warmth of friends to follow God's lead to an unknown land and to follow God's dream instead of his own. Granted, God's dream was incredible: Abraham was to become the friend of God and the human father of God's chosen people, a great nation, a nation through which the world would be blessed.

All Abraham had to do was turn loose of his past, his dreams, his doubts, and his fears so he could trust God for his future. The almighty God wanted to become Abraham's security, his protector, his guide, his personal friend.

With God's promise tucked away in his heart, Abraham and all his family, including his father, Terah, moved from Ur and headed for the land of Canaan. They settled in the river city of Haran until Terah died. Then Abraham, his wife, Sarah, his nephew, Lot, and all his entourage left that city of trade, and at seventy-five, Abraham headed southwestward by caravan into the desert toward God's promised land. Thus began the story of his remarkable relationship with God.

Reflection: God didn't thrust a list of demands upon Abraham like a distant tyrant. By introducing himself as a friend, God provided Abraham with a relationship, a hand-in-hand demonstration of his desires and concerns, his limits and his love for his people. The goal of this journey into the promised land wasn't just a place to live; it was also a way to live—in a closer relationship with God.

Our friendship with God begins, just as Abraham's did, with risk, shared time, and trust. The benefits are spectacular—God receives the glory and we receive his love. Imagine a God who wants to be your friend. How could it get better than that?

"Abraham believed God, and God accepted Abraham's faith, and that faith made him right with God." And Abraham was called God's friend.

JAMES 2:23

Becoming
Abraham's God

Abraham and Sarah spent most of their lives roaming the land of God's promise. They traveled like pilgrims from one end of it to the other, building altars, living in tents, raising cattle, and waiting for a son. After all, how could Abraham father a great nation without at least one son?

God renewed his promise to Abraham in the form of a covenant—a sealed agreement. Abraham's descendants would be as numerous as the stars of heaven, and their land would include everything between the Nile River in Egypt and the Euphrates River in Babylon. As important as the land was, the most important part of the covenant was the promised relationship. God would be Abraham's God and the God of Abraham's descendants. Abraham was to keep himself faithful to God as were his descendants.

With this promise to Abraham, the Almighty committed himself to an extraordinary, heart-to-heart relationship with one of his creations. For Abraham, God was as close as a friend but with the guidance and perspective of a father. The relationship between God and Abraham was the only part of God's promise that was completely fulfilled in Abraham's lifetime.

Reflection: God not only became the God of Abraham and his descendants, he became Abraham's friend. This was an unprecedented relationship. Friendship is difficult enough between equals but unheard of between creature and creator.

With unshakable promises, God still covenants to have a relationship with his creatures. And he demands the same response from us that he required of Abraham—trust.

"I will make an agreement between me and you and all your descendants from now on: I will be your God and the God of all your descendants. You live in the land of Canaan now as a stranger, but I will give you and your descendants all this land forever. And I will be the God of your descendants."

GENESIS 17:7–8

Abraham felt sure that God was able to do what he had promised. So, "God accepted Abraham's faith, and that faith made him right with God."

ROMANS 4:21–22

God loves to provide

A braham was ninety-nine years old when God told him he was about to be a father, and Abraham laughed. A few days later, while Abraham was providing food and shelter to three strangers, God told him that within the year Sarah would give birth to a son. Sarah overheard the words and laughed. In what appears an expression of God's sense of humor, God told them to name their coming son "Isaac," which means "laughter."

Finally Abraham and Sarah had a son—the promised son. But it wasn't Abraham and Sarah's fertility that produced Isaac; it was God's gracious planning. In Sarah's pregnancy, God did at least two things. He kept his promise of descendants, and he helped his chosen couple to see beyond their own vision—he helped them trust him for the impossible.

Reflection: Abraham and Sarah got to see a side of God that few people can imagine—his sense of humor. God appears to have delighted in announcing the long-awaited birth and must have laughed a little himself when he told them to name the boy "laughter." Can't you see God chuckling to himself, while doing the impossible in Abraham and Sarah's lives?

God still sees our misgivings, still senses our feelings and worries before we have words to express them, and at times still surprises us with his sense of humor.

He was too old to have children, and Sarah could not have children. It was by faith that Abraham was made able to become a father, because he trusted God to do what he had promised. This man was so old he was almost dead, but from him came as many descendants as there are stars in the sky. Like the sand on the seashore, they could not be counted.

Hebrews 11:11–12

Face to face with God

While Abraham was still basking in the news of a coming son, God shared his plans to destroy the notoriously wicked cities of Sodom and Gomorrah. Abraham was immediately concerned, since his nephew Lot was living there at the time. With cautious audacity Abraham bargained for the fate of the cities. The creature dared to reason with the Creator, and the Creator was willing to listen. Abraham asked God if he would destroy the cities if fifty good people could be found there. God agreed to spare the cities if fifty good people could be found. Like negotiators searching for common ground, Abraham haggled with God from fifty, to forty-five, to forty, to thirty, to twenty, to ten. Abraham stopped there, not daring to go any farther. Ultimately, ten good people could not be found, and after Lot and his family were rescued, God totally destroyed the corrupt cities of Sodom and Gomorrah.

The conversation was unprecedented and striking. The tent-dwelling, altar-building, promise-believing man from Ur stood nervously toe to toe with his God, and God allowed it. Not only did he allow it, he was willing to modify the plans of heaven at Abraham's request.

Reflection: God not only shared his plan with Abraham, he even allowed Abraham to stand toe to toe, eye to eye and humbly challenge him. This open, straightforward approach to God is assuring. God allows his people to learn more about his actions and concerns and intentions, even if our knowledge comes as a result of questioning. God listens and takes our concerns seriously.

The LORD said, "Should I tell Abraham what I am going to do now?...

"I have heard many complaints against the people of Sodom and Gomorrah. They are very evil. I will go down and see if they are as bad as I have heard...."

Abraham stood there before the LORD. Then Abraham approached him and asked,... "Surely you will not destroy the good people along with the evil ones.... You are the judge of all the earth. Won't you do what is right?"...

Then Abraham said, "Though I am only dust and ashes, I have been brave to speak to the Lord."

GENESIS 18:17–27

Tested by crisis

Just as God promised, Isaac, the long-awaited son, was born. Abraham and Sara must have been grateful parents, and they surely spent many days with Isaac, enjoying the blessings of God's watchful care.

Although God had also promised that Abraham's descendants would inherit the land of Canaan, at that time it was possessed by others. These people lived by their own rules and in the name of religion did repulsive things; they even sacrificed their firstborn sons to please their gods. So when God asked Abraham to take his son, Isaac, to Moriah and offer him as a sacrifice, it wasn't a total shock.

Abraham's trust in God, based on years of devotion, was so strong that he took Isaac to Moriah, built an altar, tied Isaac on the altar, and raised his knife, preparing to kill his son, fully confident that his God would bring Isaac back to life. God stopped Abraham, provided another sacrifice, and reaffirmed his promise. Abraham's God didn't require the sacrifice of first-borns, but he did want his people to believe in him and his power, to trust his promises, to depend on his care, and to obey his instructions. He wanted to know they were loyal, whether his commands made sense to them or not.

Reflection: Faith is always tested by crisis. God will ask whatever competes for our hearts to be laid on the altar as he seeks the best for our future, our growth, and our relationship with him.

It was by faith that Abraham, when God tested him, offered his son Isaac as a sacrifice. God made the promises to Abraham, but Abraham was ready to offer his own son as a sacrifice. God had said, "The descendants I promised you will be from Isaac." Abraham believed that God could raise the dead, and really, it was as if Abraham got Isaac back from death.

HEBREWS 11:17–19

The pain of death

Sarah lived long enough to see Isaac grow into a strong young man. Then at the age of 127, she died. Abraham bought a plot of land with the cave of Machpelah on it, and in that hillside cemetery Abraham buried Sarah.

Abraham and Sarah had been partners on an incredible journey since their days in Ur, and their shared travels had brought them a closeness that caused Abraham to mourn deeply at her death. God tells of Abraham's sadness and his desire to bury Sarah's body, and for the first time God tells of the tears connected with physical death. God didn't take away Abraham's sadness, but God is the God of all comfort.

When Abraham died many years later, he was buried with Sarah in the cave of Machpelah. In spite of never laying claim to any land but a burial plot, Abraham had walked from river to river in the promised land, forging a profound companionship with the God of promise.

God's family was born of courageous and faithful stock, and the God of Abraham must have been pleased with this man he described as a friend.

Reflection: Our struggle with death is an inevitable part of the human experience. God knows our fears, our sorrow, our loneliness, and although he does not shield us from pain, for that is part of life after the Garden, he stays close by, shares our burden, and gives us hope and comfort.

The death of one that belongs to the LORD
is precious in his sight.

PSALM 116:15

God is the Father who is full of mercy and all comfort.

2 CORINTHIANS 1:3

Man's schemes, God's wisdom

Before Abraham died, he sent a trusted servant back to his brother's family in Haran to select a wife for Isaac. The aging father didn't want Isaac marrying a woman from Canaan. So God guided the servant to Rebekah, and when the servant and Rebekah returned to Canaan, Isaac married her and loved her very much.

Isaac kept the traditions of his father. He, too, was a prosperous, nomadic herdsman. He, too, received the promise of relationship with God and the legacy of the land. The son of Abraham seems to have been a peaceable man who spent much of his life retracing the steps of his father, redigging the wells his father had dug, and following the God his father had followed.

After twenty years without children, Isaac prayed for Rebekah, and she became pregnant with twins. When she grew concerned about the constant struggling in her womb, God told her two nations were inside her and that the older brother would end up serving the younger. When the babies were born, Isaac and Rebekah named the first boy Esau and the second Jacob (loosely translated "trickster").

There must have been times when the boys sat around the fire in the evening, listening to their father tell stories about their grandfather and their God. Their family had a great heritage and a God-ordained destiny, but neither son seemed to depend much on God. Esau got so hungry one day he traded his birthright—the position of family guide and priest—to

Jacob for a bowl of soup. Jacob, eager to secure the blessings, took advantage of the situation to insure his own future. Despite the faith of their fathers, Jacob and Esau relied on themselves rather than God, but even their scheming served to further God's plans.

Reflection: Closeness with God is non-transferable; it can't be handed down from generation to generation. Fathers and mothers can lead their children toward God and teach them about God, but they can't force their children to follow him. God doesn't force his children to follow him, and as parents we cannot either. We can, however, learn from how God deals with his children in both the good and bad times, and we can take comfort in his ability to redeem any situation.

Before the two boys were born, God told Rebekah, "The older will serve the younger." This was before the boys had done anything good or bad. God said this so that the one chosen would be chosen because of God's own plan. He was chosen because he was the one God wanted to call, not because of anything he did.

ROMANS 9:11–12

The transforming power

When it was time for Isaac to give his sons their blessing—the father's vision of their futures—Rebekah and Jacob tricked blind Isaac into giving Jacob the blessing reserved for the oldest. Rather than give God a chance to work out the prophecy he had given Rebekah, they manipulated Isaac so his unalterable blessing would go to Jacob. When Esau discovered what they had done, he was furious and wanted to kill Jacob. To escape the anger of his brother, Jacob was sent to Haran to find a wife, and he left home with nothing but his staff, a walking stick. Jacob now possessed the birthright and the blessing but at the cost of his family and his home.

It didn't take long for God to get this lonely traveler's attention. In the middle of a restless dream, God took this unpromising young man and gave him a promise—the same promise he had given Abraham. Isaac's old stories about Abraham's journey with God must have prepared Jacob for this dramatic encounter, but it was Jacob's own brokenness that opened his heart to God's presence.

The next morning Jacob named that place "Bethel," meaning "the house of God." Feeling as if he was standing at the gateway to heaven, a humbled Jacob offered his own modest promise in response to God's extravagant offer. He said yes to the God of his heritage. Bethel became an anchor point in Jacob's life. He left committed to God and confident that someday God would restore his family.

Reflection: Our God is in the transformation business. He doesn't just recover and reclaim us; he restores, revives, and renews. He never leaves us trapped in our weaknesses and failures but instead keeps shaping and molding us as long as we let him. His focus is always on where we're headed, not where we've been.

When Jacob awoke from his sleep, he thought, "Surely the LORD is in this place, and I was not aware of it."...

Then Jacob made a vow, saying, "If God will be with me and will watch over me on this journey I am taking and will give me food to eat and clothes to wear so that I return safely to my father's house, then the LORD will be my God and this stone that I have set up as a pillar will be God's house, and of all that you give me I will give you a tenth."

GENESIS 28:16–22, NIV

Wrestling with God

In Haran, Jacob worked for Laban, Rebekah's brother, who proved to be just as much a manipulator as Jacob had been. But after twenty years God had blessed Jacob with Rachel and Leah as wives, eleven sons, servants, and enormous flocks. According to God's calendar, it was now time for Jacob to return to Canaan.

When Jacob's caravan reached the borders of Canaan, he was warned that Esau was on his way to meet him. Fearful of his brother's intentions, Jacob turned to God. He thanked God for staying with him in Haran and blessing him; then he begged God to save him and his family from the revenge of Esau. Jacob sent a peace offering ahead, hoping to pacify his brother.

That night Jacob wrestled with an angel and endured until morning. When it was over, Jacob was convinced he had seen the face of God and lived to tell about it. The result gave Jacob new confidence and a new name—a new way to see himself. No longer was he to be known as the "trickster;" now he was to be called "Israel"—the "struggler."

His reunion with Esau was nothing like he had imagined. God blessed them with reconciliation, and later Jacob built the first altar named after the God of Israel. The door to God's promise finally swung wide open—Israel had twelve sons.

Reflection: At some point in our lives we all identify with the wrestling Jacob. We wrestle with God in a search for truth — truth about our world, our faith, and ourselves. Thankfully God is a self-restrained wrestling partner who seeks our growth, not our defeat. May we, like Jacob, hear God say, "You have wrestled with God and with people, and you have won."

The man said, "Your name will no longer be Jacob. Your name will now be Israel, because you have wrestled with God and with people, and you have won."

GENESIS 32:28

You support me with your right hand.
You have stooped to make me great.
You give me a better way to live,
so I live as you want me to.

PSALM 18:35–36

LORD, I trust you.
I have said, "You are my God."
My life is in your hands.

PSALM 31:14–15

Testing man's integrity

Sometime during these years, God and Satan had a conversation concerning Job, a wealthy and wise man of God who lived in the region east of Canaan. Satan asked to shatter Job's world, believing he would curse God, and God allowed Satan to do so. In a single day this influential man lost everything—his wealth, his servants, and all ten of his children. Then ugly boils covered his body, and this once highly respected man found himself confined to the local ash heap. His wife suggested he curse God and die. His friends explained that since God is just, bad things happen to bad people and good things happen to good people. They believed Job must have done something terrible and he had to confess and repent. But Job was incensed at their assumptions and judgments. He was innocent and still suffering.

Job recounted how close he and God used to be, and he was angry and bewildered by the changes. In his pain Job cried out for God. He prayed to die. He wished he had never been born. He asked God to give him an answer.

Finally, God spoke for himself, and Job was hushed by God's litany of questions and overwhelmed by God's greatness. Job's view of God had been myopic. All the suffering, all the losses, and all the speculation faded into the background. Job felt insignificant but confirmed, unworthy but blessed. After all, he had seen and heard God himself. God had shown himself to be the Almighty God, and that was enough.

Job's integrity was intact—although he questioned, he never cursed God. In the spiritual world Job was unaware of, he had provided God with a victory over Satan, and God blessed Job more than ever. His health and wealth returned. His wife gave birth to ten more children, and they had children, and they had children, and they had children. He lived to see four generations and died 140 years later.

Reflection: In this unjust world, a life of integrity depends on trusting God even when we don't understand him. Fact is, we won't make a single promise or hold a single conviction that won't be tested; Satan sees to that. The question is, will our courage match our commitment?

The secret of maintaining our integrity is to keep our eyes focused beyond our suffering, failures, and pain on the dazzling, glorious greatness of our God, who remains constant and trustworthy. When we can say with all our heart, "God, if I suffer or die, I will suffer or die giving glory to you. If I live, I will live giving glory to you. Either way I'm trusting you," then we are a tiny step closer to the Almighty.

On another day the angels came to present themselves before the LORD, and Satan also came with them to present himself before him. And the LORD said to Satan, "Where have you come from?"

Satan answered the LORD, "From roaming through the earth and going back and forth in it."

Then the LORD said to Satan, "Have you considered my servant Job? There is no one on earth like him; he is blameless and upright, a man who fears God and shuns evil. And he still maintains his integrity, though you incited me against him to ruin him without any reason."…

[Job's] wife said to him, "Are you still holding on to your integrity? Curse God and die!"

He replied, "…Shall we accept good from God, and not trouble?"

In all this, Job did not sin in what he said.

JOB 2:1–10, NIV

Trusting in God's presence

God had blessed Israel with two wives and twelve sons, but Israel's sons had trouble getting along with one another. Because Joseph was born to Israel in his old age, Israel openly favored him, inciting the other brothers' hatred. In a fit of jealousy, Joseph's quarreling brothers sold him into slavery and then told Isaac he had been devoured by a wild animal. The man who had deceived his father was now deceived by his own sons. Although the seventeen-year-old Joseph was on his way to Egypt in chains, God had a plan for Joseph, a journey that would take him from the pit to power. And God would be with him every step of the way.

God and Joseph forged a trustworthy relationship. God was with Joseph as he served in the house of Potiphar. God was with him when he was falsely accused and sent to prison. God gave Joseph the ability to bless the people he came in contact with there. Eventually God gave Joseph the successful interpretation of Pharaoh's dreams, and at thirty years of age Joseph was appointed second in command of all Egypt, because it was part of God's plan not only to rescue Joseph but his chosen people.

When a seven-year famine swept the land, Egypt was the only place people could buy grain. Among the early buyers Joseph recognized his own brothers, but they didn't recognize him. God had healed Joseph's resentment toward his brothers, and his heart was overwhelmed at their presence. However, Joseph wanted to know if they had changed their ways. Had they repented, or were they still untrustworthy? So he set up an elaborate plan to see if they would abandon their younger brother Benjamin, as they had abandoned him years before. When Joseph learned that they had changed, that they would not abandon their brother, he could hold back no longer, and he gave his brothers the surprise of their lives. He told them who he was.

They were all alive because God had been at work. He had used the brothers' spiteful actions to fulfill a plan that was beyond their ability to know.

Joseph moved the whole family to Egypt and was reunited with his father, his brothers, and their families.

Reflection: Despite his own brothers turning against him, Joseph refused to be entangled by resentment. He refused to think himself a victim, blaming others for his circumstances. Instead, he trusted the ever-present God, and over and over again in Joseph's story, we find the words "the Lord was with Joseph." What the brothers meant for evil, God used for good—for Joseph, his brothers, and for the nations he saved from starvation. As we put our trust in God and let go of our resentment or bitterness, God can work through us also to implement his plans on earth.

When the brothers came close to him, he said to them, "I am your brother Joseph, whom you sold as a slave to go to Egypt. Now don't be worried or angry with yourselves because you sold me here. God sent me here ahead of you to save people's lives…and to keep you alive in an amazing way. So it was not you who sent me here, but God."

GENESIS 45:4–8

Trust the LORD with all your
    heart,
  and don't depend on your
    own understanding.
Remember the LORD in all you
    do,
  and he will give you success.

Don't depend on your own
    wisdom.
  Respect the LORD and refuse
    to do wrong.
Then your body will be healthy,
  and your bones will be strong.

PROVERBS 3:5–8

Called by God

Numbering barely seventy-five when Israel's family arrived in Egypt, within four hundred years Israel's descendants had grown to more than a million people. Eventually an Egyptian king rose to power who had no knowledge of Joseph, and he made the descendants, whom they called Hebrews, into slaves. Fearing their potential strength, the Egyptians worked the Hebrews mercilessly, and as their numbers grew, so did the oppression.

God was not deaf to their cries, however. God chose a Hebrew infant named Moses to grow up to lead his people out of Egypt and into the land promised to Abraham, Isaac, and Jacob. Under God's watchful eye, Moses was raised in Pharaoh's palace and given all the benefits of royalty. But when he was forty years old, he killed an Egyptian who was beating one of the Hebrews and ended up running for his life and losing himself in the desert. For the next forty years, the chosen deliverer of God's people lived the primitive life of a shepherd in the Sinai wilderness.

On one of those run-of-the-mill shepherding days at the foot of Mount Sinai, Moses happened upon a most unusual sight—a flaming bush that refused to burn up. As he walked closer, the puzzled shepherd heard God calling his name from the bush. God asked Moses to take off his sandals because he was standing in God's presence on holy ground. God didn't want anything—not even sandal leather—to come between them. Then the almighty God introduced himself not only as the God of Abraham, Isaac, and Jacob but as the I AM God—the God who was and is and is to come.

Even though it would be years before Moses would be able to see it, everything that had happened to him up to that moment had prepared him for God's call. God was about to reach down into the oppression of Egypt and rescue the descendants of Israel and lead them home to the land he had promised their ancestors. This humble shepherd was God's handpicked deliverer—the director of God's relocation project.

Uncertain that the king of Egypt or even the leaders of Israel would listen to him, Moses balked. But for every "what if…" Moses raised, God had a "do this…." In fact, God provided his hesitant leader with everything needed for the task—God's powerful, personal presence and a transformed staff full of surprises. Moses had no more excuses. By accepting God's call, he was thrust out of a wilderness of obscurity and into a powerful partnership with the I AM God.

Reflection: God transformed more than Moses' staff. He gave his partner new vision, a new mission, and new resources. By accepting God's invitation, eighty-year-old Moses came out of retirement, not because he wanted it, but because the I AM God wanted it.

God has plans for everybody: projects, opportunities, responsibilities, tasks, and callings, and he doesn't allow anything to come

The LORD said, "I have seen the troubles my people have suffered in Egypt, and I have heard their cries when the Egyptian slave masters hurt them. I am concerned about their pain, and I have come down to save them from the Egyptians…. So now I am sending you to the king of Egypt. Go! Bring my people, the Israelites, out of Egypt!"

But Moses said to God, "I am not a great man! How can I go to the king and lead the Israelites out of Egypt?"

God said, "I will be with you…."

Moses said to God, "…What if the people say, 'What is his name?' What should I tell them?"

Then God said to Moses, "I AM WHO I AM." When you go to the people of Israel, tell them, 'I AM sent me to you.'"

God also said to Moses, "This is what you should tell the people: 'The LORD is the God of your ancestors—the God of Abraham, the God of Isaac, and the God of Jacob. He sent me to you.' This will always be my name, by which people from now on will know me."

EXODUS 3:7–15

53

between him and his called person. So, take off your mask, check your fears, admit your inadequacies, accept the call, and get ready for your own encounter on holy ground. You are a child of the present-tense God who knows your past and, in spite of it, invites you into a future with him. He is still the I AM God, and his promise remains, "I am with you."

I look up to the hills,
　　but where does my help come from?
My help comes from the LORD,
　　who made heaven and earth.

He will not let you be defeated.
　　He who guards you never sleeps.
He who guards Israel
　　never rests or sleeps.
The LORD guards you.
　　The LORD is the shade that protects you from the sun.
The sun cannot hurt you during the day,
　　and the moon cannot hurt you at night.
The LORD will protect you from all dangers;
　　he will guard your life.
The LORD will guard you as you come and go,
　　both now and forever.

PSALM 121

God rescues and renews

Moses returned to Egypt and told the leaders of Israel that the I AM God of Abraham, Isaac, and Jacob had sent him to liberate them, but it took a host of surprises from Moses' staff and miracles straight from the hand of God before the people had confidence in Moses and before the king agreed to release them. Finally, just as God had said, they were free to leave—to go home. God's mobile nation was born. It was an incredible day, a day God wanted the Israelites to remember forever, a day he would anchor in their memories by the Passover Feast.

More than a million freed Hebrew slaves eagerly followed Moses eastward out of Egypt, while the locals gave them gifts and hurried them on their way. God watched over their journey and led them with a perpetual cloud during the day and fire in the sky at night. The God they had prayed to for generations, the God who had seemed distant and silent, was now present and powerful and prominent. After their 430 years in Egypt, he was taking his people home, and with them they carried Joseph's bones.

Staff in hand, Moses led his new nation to the Red Sea. In the meantime the Egyptian king had changed his mind and had sent his chariots after them. When the Israelites found themselves trapped between shores of the Red Sea and the thundering Egyptian chariots in the distance, they panicked, but Moses stood strong. He stretched out his staff, and God split the sea from one side to the other, all the way to the bottom, so the Israelites could cross the sea on dry land. When the Egyptians tried to follow them across the sea bottom, God collapsed the walls of water, and the Egyptian forces were totally destroyed. With mighty demonstrations of power and preeminence, the I AM God rescued his people just as he had promised.

Reflection: For generations God's people had suffered and cried for relief. When God was ready, he did much more than relieve their suffering, however; he won their freedom. God's people must have been filled with joyful emotions that had been buried for a lifetime. In a sense they were new people. Anytime God rescues a person, his life is changed. The old is gone, and the new is filled with joy.

God's people were the objects of the most sensational, miraculous rescue in the history of the world. And the exodus was just the beginning.

Now this is what the LORD says.
He created you, people of Jacob;
  he formed you, people of Israel.
He says, "Don't be afraid, because
    I have saved you.
  I have called you by name,
    and you are mine.
When you pass through the
    waters, I will be with you.
  When you cross rivers, you
    will not drown.
When you walk through fire, you
    will not be burned,
  nor will the flames hurt you.
This is because I, the LORD, am
    your God,
  the Holy One of Israel, your
    Savior.

ISAIAH 43:1–3

Learning to trust the I Am God

God wanted his people to experience hope, to enjoy his blessings, to become a great nation—one that would bless other nations around the world, forever. The task was enormous, but God had been working on Israel long before Egypt enslaved them. Everything he did for them centered on making them into a holy nation, suited for his purposes. They had but one task—to learn to trust a God they didn't know.

God's dramatic rescue of the Israelites from Egypt was followed by more signs and wonders. God's people camped in the desert, eating food miraculously bestowed from heaven, drinking water from rocks, following a strange cloud in the daytime and a pillar of fire at night. Day after day God dazzled them with his power, provision, and protection, but they still didn't know him.

Three months after they left Egypt, God's nation arrived at Mount Sinai. Moses gathered Israel around the foot of the mountain so God could speak to them. The anticipation must have been fierce. How could they forget the deaths in Egypt, their dramatic hike between walls of water, the drowning of the Egyptians? These apprehensive slaves had seen that Moses' God could just as easily destroy them as talk to them. The people were convinced that Moses knew God; now they too were going to hear him speak. What if he turned against them?

The all-powerful I AM God descended from heaven shrouded in fire, punctuated with thunder and lightning. A monstrous trumpet blast announced his presence, and the ground shook. The people trembled with fear and begged for him to stop. They were too afraid to hear God for themselves. So Moses became Israel's ears and God's spokesman, the first of God's prophets. He spent weeks inside the clouds on Mount Sinai, talking with God. And the people later listened to Moses as he repeated God's commands.

Reflection: God had set out to build an exemplary nation from a frightened collection of freed slaves. They had done nothing to earn it—God did it. And to initiate his relationship he promised his love, his presence, and his protection. But they were petrified, and ears of stone don't hear well. It wasn't God's intention that his people be disabled by his voice; he wanted them to be a nation of priests—people with a direct line to him, people who understood him to be the Almighty and the One who cared enough to provide for their daily needs. What God wanted from the Israelites is what he wants from us today— respect and obedience.

The LORD...said, "...Tell the people of Israel: 'Every one of you has seen what I did to the people of Egypt. You saw how I carried you out of Egypt, as if on eagle's wings. And I brought you here to me. So now if you obey me and keep my agreement, you will be my own possession, chosen from all nations. Even though the whole earth is mine, you will be my kingdom of priests and a holy nation.'"

EXODUS 19:3–6

When the people heard the thunder and the trumpet, and when they saw the lightning and the smoke rising from the mountain, they shook with fear and stood far away from the mountain. Then they said to Moses, "Speak to us yourself, and we will listen. But don't let God speak to us, or we will die."

Then Moses said to the people, "Don't be afraid, because God has come to test you. He wants you to respect him so you will not sin."

EXODUS 20:18–20

Accepting the covenant of love

God embraced the Israelites, not because they were numerous, or good, or strong; he chose them solely because he loved them. He was willing to risk his love because of a promise he had made to Abraham, Isaac, and Jacob. He descended to the mountain to become their God, to introduce himself to them. He offered these freed but frightened slaves the relationship above all relationships. Nothing like this had ever happened on earth.

God's mountaintop manifesto can be summed up in two bottom-line demands—love God and love people. God asked that his new nation do more than serve him and worship him; he asked that they love him. He wanted more than obedient behavior; he wanted surrendered hearts. The almighty God of creation, the promise-keeping God of Abraham, Isaac, and Jacob, the eternal-storehouse-of-blessing God of Job, the I-AM-with-you God of Moses risked his reputation on these stubborn and forgetful people because he loved them. And he wanted them to learn to love him.

Without hesitation the Israelites promised their allegiance to God—to be God's people. Then God and Israel's leaders met together on the mountain, celebrating their agreement, their covenant, and the beginning of what would prove to be a constantly vacillating relationship.

Reflection: God chose to build his nation on love, not on military might, or individual rights, or a democratic political system. In fact, his whole concept of religion was new; it was designed by God, not man. God did everything first—he accepted the people right where they were and loved them unconditionally, while they struggled to learn how to love him.

God's love is alluring, captivating, and contagious, filling that spiritual yearning deep within our hearts. Based on his divine commitment, God loves us, understands our struggles, and forgives our failures. He is the perfect father whom we seek to know, to serve, and to love, because he first loved us.

Moses told the people all the LORD's words and laws for living. Then all of the people answered out loud together, "We will do all the things the LORD has said." So Moses wrote down all the words of the LORD.... He set up twelve stones, one stone for each of the twelve tribes of Israel.... Then he took the Book of the Agreement and read it so the people could hear him. And they said, "We will do everything that the LORD has said; we will obey."...

Moses, Aaron, Nadab, Abihu, and seventy of the older leaders of Israel went up the mountain and saw the God of Israel.... These leaders of the Israelites saw God, but God did not destroy them. Then they ate and drank together.

EXODUS 24:3–11

Jesus answered, "'Love the Lord your God with all your heart, all your soul, and all your mind.' This is the first and most important command. And the second command is like the first: 'Love your neighbor as you love yourself.'"

MATTHEW 22:37–39

Learning to live God's way

While they were camped around Sinai, God gave his people much more than ten commandments; he endowed them with laws to guide every part of life. God's own decrees of love and limits shaped the development of morality and personal character. He provided Israel with standards of right and wrong—further defining good and evil. God set up civil laws and provided ready-made cultural mores. He set standards for community health, for legal judgments, for farming, for funerals, and marriage and family concerns. He thought of everything, including traditions, rituals, feasts, worship practices, and specific laws for how to treat the poor, the weak, and the strangers. God provided the best.

God's promises are rock solid, but his people's promises proved much easier to make than to keep. The people were slow to learn and quick to devalue God's commands; in short order, they failed to keep their part of the agreement. They turned their backs on God's leadership and trusted their own abilities and plans. Each time they violated God's laws, or ignored his commands, they faced his discipline—his corrective consequences.

The thundering God on the mountain, the God who ordained laws, became the God of the wilderness, the God of training. God used every experience of life, even consequences, to help his new nation learn how to be the best they could be.

Reflection: God's national standards provided specifics for how to please and love the holy, almighty God. There never was a time, however, when people were able to keep all the rules, to do everything perfectly. Yet over and over Moses told the people to obey and to love the Lord. Either alone — love or obedience — was hollow. Together, even in their imperfection, God was pleased.

In the future when your children ask you, "What is the meaning of the laws, commands, and rules the LORD our God gave us?" tell them, "…The LORD brought us out of Egypt to lead us here and to give us the land he promised our ancestors. The LORD ordered us to obey all these commands and to respect the LORD our God so that we will always do well and stay alive, as we are today. The right thing for us to do is this: Obey all these rules in the presence of the LORD our God, as he has commanded."…

So know that the LORD your God is God, the faithful God. He will keep his agreement of love for a thousand lifetimes for people who love him and obey his commands.

DEUTERONOMY 6:20–25; 7:9

Access to God

To assure the people of his continual presence, God instructed them to build him a dwelling place, a holy tent or tabernacle, a home for his abiding presence. No longer did Moses go up on Mount Sinai to meet with God; God came down in the midst of the camp, covering the tabernacle with a cloud and filling it with his presence.

The men of Aaron's family were chosen to serve as priests, and God selected Aaron to be the first high priest—the man charged with interceding for the unfaithful people with their faithful God. The men in Aaron's family handled all the details concerning worship, sacrifices, and the tabernacle itself, including the symbol of God's presence—the holy box called the Ark of the Covenant.

Specific holy days were scheduled each year. One of them was the Day of Atonement, an annual time of remorse and repentance, a time to cleanse the soul. On that day Aaron killed a young goat and offered its death as a substitute for the death that all the people deserved. The ritual called for him to take the blood of the animal into the holiest place in the tabernacle— the place of God's presence.

Aaron would also take a live goat and confess over it all the sins of the people—all their failures, stubbornness, forgetfulness, and their outright defiance of God. Then the scapegoat was led into the desert, never to be seen again, symbolically taking the sins of the people with it. All this was designed by God as a way to cleanse his unholy people and keep them in relationship with a holy God.

Reflection: God knew his people would have trouble living up to his standards and would set their own markers far short of their agreement with him. Without the priests constantly bringing the people back into relationship with God, without the annual holy days and daily sacrifices reminding the people of their failures and God's blessings, without leaders like Moses, this burgeoning nation would never remain faithful.

Sin—our failure to be what God created us to be—separates us from God. But God has continually made a way for us to come back to him and to commune with him, because nothing is more important to the Father than his relationship with his children.

Happy is the person
  whose sins are forgiven,
  whose wrongs are pardoned.
Happy is the person
  whom the LORD does not
    consider guilty
  and in whom there is nothing
    false.

When I kept things to myself.
  I felt weak deep inside me.
  I moaned all day long.
Day and night you punished me.
  My strength was gone as in the
    summer heat.
Then I confessed my sins to you
  and didn't hide my guilt.
I said, "I will confess my sins to
    the LORD,"
  and you forgave my guilt.

For this reason, all who obey you
  should pray to you while they
    still can.
When troubles rise like a flood,
  they will not reach them.
You are my hiding place.
  You protect me from my
    troubles
  and fill me with songs of salvation.

PSALM 32:1–7

65

The discipline and mercy of God

When it came time to move from Sinai toward the promised land, God's people followed wherever his cloud led them. But before long, their praise of God turned to a spirit of ingratitude. When they reached the southern edge of Canaan, a team of twelve men was sent on a forty-day mission to gather information about the land and its inhabitants. They returned with a mixed report. The land held bounty beyond their hopes but also powerful inhabitants. Ten of the twelve men saw certain defeat. Following their lead, the people cowered in fear, ready to kill Moses and return to Egypt. It was like slapping God in the face.

God was ready to destroy these self-centered, unfaithful people, but Moses intervened. He appealed to God on their behalf, and God was moved. Instead of destroying his people, he disciplined them severely. Because of their lack of trust in him, they were banned from the promised land and confined to the desert for forty years, giving them lots of time to think about their rejection of God. Because of their sin, God kept them in the desert long enough to bury the generation who had lived in Egypt. Then he led their sons and daughters into the promised homeland.

Reflection: The people possibly never knew the times Moses saved them from God's judgment. Moses' relationship with God, like Abraham's, allowed him to speak one-on-one with the Almighty and seek a change in his plans. Although God seldom rescues his people from the consequences of their behavior, he never fails to forgive their guilt when they turn back to him. He is the perfect image of a father who disciplines, forgives, and accepts his children with a tender, understanding heart, and he is always available to those who listen to his call and his claim on their lives.

Then Moses said to the LORD, "'...The LORD doesn't become angry quickly, but he has great love. He forgives sin and law breaking. But the LORD never forgets to punish guilty people....' By your great love, forgive these people's sin, just as you have forgiven them from the time they left Egypt until now."

The LORD answered, "I have forgiven them as you asked. But, as surely as I live and as surely as my glory fills the whole earth, I make this promise: All these men saw my glory and the miracles I did in Egypt and in the desert, but they disobeyed me and tested me ten times. So not one of them will see the land I promised to their ancestors. No one who rejected me will see that land."

NUMBERS 14:13, 18–23

67

Reaching the promised land

After forty years in the desert, the Israelites again came to the southern door of the promised land, but it was time for a change in leadership. Moses was at the end of his life, and many new challenges lay ahead for God's nation. Before the baton of leadership was passed to Joshua, Moses reminded the people of their covenant agreement with God. Moses knew the people well; he warned them that when they settled into their new houses and grew comfortable in their new land they would forget their God who had provided it all. He knew these people would once again grow more complacent and self-reliant and less aware of God's presence, and less willing to keep their agreement with God. In the midst of their excitement about their new homeland, Moses was deeply concerned about their ability to remember whose they were.

In an attempt to protect them one final time, Moses spent his last days preaching passionate sermons, reminding them of God's deliverance, singing a ballad of hope, blessing their journey, and asking them to renew their covenant with God. Then, after he blessed each of the twelve families of Israel, Moses hiked his last mountain—this time Mount Nebo. From here, Moses could see beyond the Jordan River into the fertile land that awaited them. After a lifetime of following the Lord on earth, Moses died in the arms of his God. He bypassed the promised land to go straight home to God.

The task of leading God's people into the land promised long ago to Abraham, Isaac, and Jacob then fell to Joshua. In a scene reminiscent of crossing the Red Sea, God held back the waters of the Jordan so his people could cross on dry land. To remind the people of God's power over the river and his provision for them, Joshua had their leaders build a memorial at Gilgal, their first campsite. The twelve rocks were to remind the parents to tell their children about how God had brought them out of Egypt, through the desert, across the Jordan, and into this place they now would call home.

And for as long as Joshua lived, the people remembered their God and their promise to him.

Reflection: Moses' final words held both promises and warnings, blessings and curses. Promises of God's bounty and protection. Promises of a land full of cities and fields for the taking. Promises of a centuries-old dream about to be fulfilled. But for this fickle nation, reaching the promised land held a new threat to their trust in God. God would be faithful, but once they became comfortable in their new land, would they remain faithful to him? When we're comfortable are we as faithful?

Look, today I offer you life and success, death and destruction. I command you today to love the LORD your God, to do what he wants you to do, and to keep his commands, his rules, and his laws. Then you will live and grow in number, and the LORD your God will bless you in the land you are entering to take as your own.

But if you turn away from the LORD and do not obey him, if you are led to bow and serve other gods, I tell you today that you will surely be destroyed. And you will not live long in the land you are crossing the Jordan River to enter and take as your own.

Today I ask heaven and earth to be witnesses. I am offering you life or death, blessings or curses. Now, choose life! Then you and your children may live. To choose life is to love the LORD your God, obey him, and stay close to him. He is your life, and he will let you live many years in the land, the land he promised to give your ancestors Abraham, Isaac, and Jacob.

DEUTERONOMY 30:15–20

69

Deciding which God to serve

Within days of Moses' death, it was clear that the God of Moses was now the God of Joshua. God renewed his promise and assured Joshua of his presence, even sending a heavenly messenger to Joshua—the commander of the Lord's armies who would go with Joshua into battle.

God was about to repossess the land and populate it with his people. In giving Israel their promised homeland, God also brought judgment on the evil ingrained in the Canaanite culture. The Canaanite worship of Baal and his lover, Ashtoreth—gods of fertility—connected sex and public lewdness with crop yields. The entire population had grown so corrupt that God ordered his new nation to destroy the Canaanites and any memory of them from the face of the earth, thereby providing his people with vacant farms and cities ready for possession while protecting them from the enticement of the Canaanites' idol worship.

As the news of the Israelites' sensational entrance into Canaan spread from city to city, the residents of Canaan grew more fearful. They had heard of the mighty God of these people and of his unrivaled power, and they were about to see his power for themselves. For six days the Israelites paraded around Jericho's walls, blowing trumpets but speechless. Then on the seventh day, God's people paraded around the walls seven times, and at the end of the last round, the trumpets blared, the people shouted, and God shook the city walls apart from top to bottom, destroying it and the protection it provided. Joshua's soldiers then climbed over the fallen stones, destroying everything in the city and claiming the victory for God.

Under God's command, Joshua led Israel on an unprecedented victory march through the land. However, after capturing and claiming the principal cities of thirty-one different kingdoms, Israel stopped. The task was not completed, but Joshua was old and tired. With God's help the people divided the land among the twelve tribes of Jacob, and from that day forward Canaan was known as Israel. But in spite of God's disapproval, some of the Canaanites and their false gods remained to haunt the Israelites for centuries.

The task of extending the borders of Israel was given to the various family territories, but it never happened, and just as God had warned, his people were soon contaminated with all the evils of idolatry. After Joshua died, the people forgot their mighty Warrior God and did whatever they pleased and worshiped any god they pleased.

"The LORD has forced many great and powerful nations to leave ahead of you. No nation has been able to defeat you. With his help, one Israelite could defeat a thousand, because the LORD your God fights for you, as he promised to do. So you must be careful to love the LORD your God.

"If you turn away from the way of the LORD and become friends with these people who are not part of Israel and marry them, the LORD your God will not help you defeat your enemies.

"...You know and fully believe that the LORD has done great things for you. You know that he has not failed to keep any of his promises. Every good promise that the LORD your God made has come true, and in the same way, his other promises will come true."

JOSHUA 23:9–15

So people have no excuse for the bad things they do. They knew God, but they did not give glory to God or thank him. Their thinking became useless. Their foolish minds were filled with darkness. They said they were wise, but they became fools. They traded the glory of God who lives forever for the worship of idols made to look like earthly people, birds, animals, and snakes.

Because they did these things, God left them and let them go their sinful way, wanting only to do evil. As a result, they became full of sexual sin, using their bodies wrongly with each other. They traded the truth of God for a lie. They worshiped and served what had been created instead of the God who created those things, who should be praised forever. Amen.

ROMANS 1:20–25

Reflection: Since the Garden of Eden, God has instructed his people to focus on *his* majesty and *his* holiness, not on their desires. Yet, on earth we have a choice. We can choose self-focused religions, which in actuality make man into a god. Or we can devote our lives to the only God beyond us, the only God who fills the yearning in our souls.

Like Israel, we are in awe of the supernatural displays of God's power and yet find it difficult to grow close to an invisible God. We are attracted to his power, because we too want power, but we opt for something less vulnerable than loving him and trusting him. After a while we become our own gods, doing what seems right in our own eyes. How tragic to spend a lifetime serving a god who is no wiser, stronger, better, or forgiving than we are.

God raises up leaders

After Joshua there was no strong leader to unite the people of Israel for over two hundred years. During this period the twelve family territories were more like loosely affiliated states than a unified nation. Even their loyalty to the almighty God who had given them the land was tenuous. Over and over again the Israelites drifted off into serving and worshiping the false gods of their neighbors. Forgetting the true God and serving these stone and wooden gods brought weakness, defeat, and oppression into their lives.

To help restore the people to him, God would raise up a leader, because he still loved his people in spite of their failures. These leaders brought Israel back to God at least seven times during these notorious years.

Some of the most unlikely people became God's instruments, among them Gideon. Gideon had heard the stories of Israel's all-powerful God, but he had experienced only hard times and the silence of God. The Israelites had turned away from God to worship Baal, so God had removed his protection and had allowed the Midianites to invade and devastate Israel.

One day Gideon was threshing his family's wheat in secret so the Midianites wouldn't seize it, when an angel found him and enlisted him to lead God's rescue operation. When Gideon questioned why God didn't show his mighty power as in the past, God responded by making hesitant Gideon into one of his most courageous leaders. (After all, God's mightiest work is always the transformation of people.)

This reluctant risktaker checked and double-checked to make sure this was actually God talking to him, and before each foray he made certain of God's presence. Gideon tore down the altars to Baal, he led three hundred brave soldiers in a rout of the Midianite army, and he won freedom for Israel. The people wanted to make him their king, but Gideon proclaimed his God as their king. God had transformed a man, rescued his people, and punished the godless Midianites.

God intervened and used his chosen leaders to rescue Israel from the corruption of false gods, and after each rescue the people would return to God and make sincere promises. But repeatedly, after several years the next generation would yield to those surrounding evil influences and turn away from God.

Reflection: Gideon's need for double-checking God wasn't so much a checking for God's will as it was a checking for his presence. Gideon knew the task, but he needed more than one assurance that God was still in the task with him. We have the same concerns, don't we? When our tasks are beyond our perceived abilities, we have difficulty trusting God to be there, to be faithful. Yet, behind the scenes he is always molding circumstances and sending us into experiences that call forth the strengths he planted in us. The amazing truth is that God is willing to continually meet us in every task and prove again and again that he is faithful. What a loving God we have.

The angel of the LORD appeared to Gideon and said, "The LORD is with you, mighty warrior!"

Then Gideon said, "Sir, if the LORD is with us, why are we having so much trouble? Where are the miracles our ancestors told us he did when the LORD brought them out of Egypt? But now he has left us and has handed us over to the Midianites."

The LORD turned to Gideon and said, "Go with your strength and save Israel from the Midianites. I am the one who is sending you."

JUDGES 6:12–14

LORD, you have examined me
   and know all about me.
You know when I sit down and
     when I get up.
   You know my thoughts before I
     think them.
You know where I go and where
     I lie down.
   You know thoroughly every-
     thing I do.
LORD, even before I say a word,
   you already know it.
You are all around me—in front
     and in back—
   and have put your hand on me.

PSALM 139:1–5

Chosen by God

While God was helping his leaders bring revival to Israel, he was also at work in the country of Moab, a longtime enemy of Israel. During a famine in Israel, an Israelite named Elimelech moved his wife and two sons to Moab, and there Elimelech died. Later, his son Kilion married a young Moabitess named Ruth, and then he also died, leaving Ruth and her mother-in-law, Naomi, as widows.

The people of Moab worshiped a horrible idol named Chemosh—a hideous-looking fire god. Ruth was likely raised worshiping this idol, but as part of Naomi's family, she had come to know something of Naomi's God, the God of Israel. While still grieving over the loss of her husband and sons, Naomi decided to return home to Bethlehem alone, but Ruth refused to leave her; she was determined to stay with this lady she had grown to love. Without concern for her own future, Ruth promised to remain with Naomi, to live among Naomi's people, and to devote herself to Naomi's God. After Naomi saw she couldn't dissuade her, the two of them made the long trek back to Bethlehem.

As soon as they arrived, Ruth did what she could to provide food for the two of them, gleaning in the fields with others who were in need. Even though she was home, Naomi was sad, but her spirits revived when she discovered that Ruth had attracted the attention of a rich landowner named Boaz, a relative of Naomi. Israelite law required close relatives to provide for widows, so Naomi instructed Ruth to appeal to Boaz for provision. It wasn't long before wedding plans were made. Ruth's devotion to Naomi's people and Naomi's God was rewarded in her lifetime and blessed future generations as she became the great-grandmother of David, the greatest king in Israel's history.

Reflection: All people are important to God. We have to go all the way back to Abraham's nephew, Lot, to connect Ruth with God's people. The people of Moab were descendants of Lot, but for generations they had forgotten the God of Abraham. Still, when Ruth turned to Naomi's God, he not only accepted her into his holy nation, he gave her a prominent place in the family's history.

God didn't choose the people of Israel because of their worth; he chose them because he loved them. And he chooses us because he loves us. God always has his eyes open, searching the earth for people who seek to know him.

Ruth said, "Don't beg me to leave you or to stop following you. Where you go, I will go. Where you live, I will live. Your people will be my people, and your God will be my God. And where you die, I will die, and there I will be buried. I ask the LORD to punish me terribly if I do not keep this promise: Not even death will separate us."

RUTH 1:16–17

"The LORD searches all the earth for people who have given themselves completely to him."

2 CHRONICLES 16:9

God calls Samuel

Among God's leaders during this time was Samuel, the last of Israel's judges. Before his birth his mother dedicated him to God's service, and when he was just a child, she took him to Shiloh to be an apprentice to the high priest of the tabernacle. Although Eli, the high priest, had constant trouble with his own evil sons, Samuel was a willing student. And God had plans for him that no one could have predicted. Samuel would, in fact, be taught by God himself.

The corruption of Eli's sons mirrored the nation itself. Many people had turned to worshiping false gods, and God had again grown displeased with his chosen people. It had been a long time since anyone had heard God's voice, and most had stopped listening. That was about to change.

Beside the glow of God's perpetual candle in the tabernacle, young Samuel lay down for the evening. Four times he was awakened by a voice calling out in the darkness—"Samuel!" At first Samuel thought it was Eli, but the voice wasn't Eli's. It was God himself, calling Samuel by name. From that night forward, God and Samuel talked often.

God had special plans for this young man. As Samuel grew into manhood, God made him into a powerful national leader, a faithful prophet, and a dependable priest.

Reflection: Imagine the heart-pounding, attention-grabbing, soul-stirring experience of hearing God's voice in the darkness—calling you by name. Has there been a time when the ears of your soul heard God call you by name? Have you ever been quiet, totally quiet, long enough to hear him? God knows our names, and he calls us into service. Not until the end of time will he force us to listen.

The LORD came and stood there and called as he had before, "Samuel, Samuel!"

Samuel said, "Speak, LORD. I am your servant and I am listening."

The LORD was with Samuel as he grew up; he did not let any of Samuel's messages fail to come true. Then all Israel, from Dan to Beersheba, knew Samuel was a true prophet of the LORD.

1 SAMUEL 3:10, 19–20

Restoring and rescuing the people

While God was shaping Samuel into an effective prophet and priest for Israel, the people continued to struggle with false gods and with the neighboring Philistines. After a crucial defeat the Israelites were stunned. Believing that God had turned his back on them, the soldiers sent for the Ark of God and had it brought to the camp. As the symbol of God's presence, they assumed the Ark would surely bring God and his blessing back to them.

However, during the next battle the Philistines captured the Ark and killed Eli's sons, the priests who had brought the Ark into battle. The Israelite soldiers who survived the battle ran away in fear, and when the news reached Eli that his sons had been killed and that the Ark had been captured, he fell over dead. It was a dark day for Israel.

At first the Philistines rejoiced. After all, they had captured the most holy article in Israel. Believing their god Dagon had given them victory, they honored him by placing the Ark in his temple. That proved to be a bad decision. Within forty-eight hours Dagon was mysteriously dismembered. Possessing the Ark brought nothing but disaster to the Philistines. Their false gods were disgraced, the people grew strangely ill, and many died. Fear filled their cities. Finally, to rid themselves of the terrors, they sent the Ark back to Israel.

For twenty years the Israelites left the Ark in the house of Abinadab as the people mourned and sought the Lord. Inspired by the preaching of Samuel, Israel began a national revival. They tore down their idols and returned humbly to the great God of their forefathers. At Samuel's request the people gathered in a great assembly at Mizpah to confess their unfaithfulness to God and to seek his favor.

While the Israelites were rallying for reconciliation, the Philistines were preparing for retaliation. Enemy soldiers swarmed down on the Israelites, ready for battle. God's people turned to Samuel; God was their only hope. Samuel prayed for rescue, and the all-powerful Warrior God of Israel responded with deafening thunder, sending the Philistines into panic and confusion. The men of Israel pursued them and defeated them.

When the battle was over, the nation of Israel was profoundly grateful to their God. Samuel set up a monument, an Ebenezer, a "stone of help," to remind the people of God's help on that day.

Reflection: The most holy piece in God's tabernacle was the Ark of God—the symbol of his presence. It wasn't an idol to be worshiped

Samuel spoke to the whole group of Israel, saying, "If you're turning back to the LORD with all your hearts, you must remove your foreign gods and your idols of Ashtoreth. You must give yourselves fully to the LORD and serve only him. Then he will save you from the Philistines."

After this happened Samuel took a stone and set it up between Mizpah and Shen. He named the stone Ebenezer, saying, "The LORD has helped us to this point."

1 SAMUEL 7:3, 12

in place of God or some magical force to be used like a charm. The Philistines, and even the Israelites, had missed the point altogether, and God held them accountable.

But when the people confessed their sins and turned back to God, once again he delivered them from their enemies. Just as they needed reminders of God's intervention, perhaps we also should set up Ebenezers to remind us of the times we have sinned and he has forgiven and rescued us.

---

1 SAMUEL 8–10; 13–15

Establishing a new kingdom

After the routing of the Philistines, Samuel began visiting key cities in Israel each year, keeping the people true to their commitment to God. Each place represented a page in Israel's history: Bethel was where Jacob struggled with God, the twelve-stone monument at Gilgal marked the crossing of the Jordan River, the Ebenezer at Mizpah reminded the people of God's recent victory over the Philistines. These were good years for Israel.

As Samuel grew older, however, the people insisted on having a king like the nations around them. They believed they needed a central government, a dynamic leader to represent them in national affairs, and a military command that could rally mighty forces in their defense. Samuel fought establishing a king as long as he could. The people's request dishonored their Protector God who had provided everything that they now took for granted. Their desire for a human king was an affront to the ruler they already had—the Almighty, the ruler of the universe.

Finally God allowed them to have a king. He selected an unknown named Saul. He had a rich heritage, the anointing of Samuel, a God-altered heart, innate ability, and a noticeable height advantage. He clearly looked the part, but something deep inside his heart kept him from playing the part.

Samuel again gathered the people at Mizpah, this time for the crowning of their king. With all the hopes of Israel on his shoulders, Saul began to unite the people of God into a kingdom.

Saul scored initial victories over Israel's enemies, but he tended to cut his own path instead of following God's lead. The brave king who began with promise became reckless, ego driven, and disconnected from God. Samuel withdrew his support and counsel, and before long God expressed his sorrow for selecting Saul to be king of Israel. Without the spirit of God in him, Saul grew paranoid and suspicious and even murderous.

Reflection: Unlike the kingdoms surrounding Israel, God's kingdom was not based on the fearfulness of the people and the fierceness of the king. God's kingdom was and is based on love and forgiveness. He wanted his people to be his subjects because they loved him, but the people continued to have trouble loving and following a king they couldn't see. They thought of kingdom in terms of territory, while God thought of kingdom in terms of hearts. God's people were totally unaware of the kingdom surrounding and enfolding them. His kingdom far exceeded any human kingdom, but the people wanted what they didn't have. They wanted to be like those they could see.

Just as the Israelites did, we tend to look at the seen—truth we can grab and hold and explain. Since we can't see the spiritual forces of God stationed all around us or the majesty and accessibility of his throne room, we want something more. Yet no human king could ever grant access as God has. We have a continuous audience before him. And once we have yielded to his rule, we are treated more like his children than subjects.

God is the King of kings, who rules over time and space, truth and justice, dreams and destinies. He has all power and majesty, glory and honor. He is king of heaven and of earth, of the seen and the unseen, of you and me. And we are his heirs.

But Samuel answered,
"What pleases the LORD more:
   burnt offerings and sacrifices
   or obedience to his voice?
It is better to obey than to sacrifice.
   It is better to listen to God than
   to offer the fat of sheep.
Disobedience is as bad as the sin
   of sorcery.
   Pride is as bad as the sin of
   worshiping idols.
You have rejected the LORD's
   command.
   Now he rejects you as king."

1 SAMUEL 15:22–23

Instilling God's dream in David's heart

Whilst Saul was still ruling Israel, God sent Samuel to anoint a new king. Samuel's journey led him to the small town of Bethlehem. He had not come to find the tallest, nor the strongest, nor the oldest of the boys of Bethlehem. He came to find God's choice. Two memorable things happened that day: God chose a young shepherd boy named David to be the next king, and Samuel learned that God doesn't judge the outward appearance but the heart.

God was pleased with David's sensitive, submissive heart, and as God had done with Saul, he had Samuel anoint David as the future king of Israel. With a few drops of oil, David found himself marked as God's anointed—his empowered representative on earth. Then, without fanfare, David returned to his father's sheep, because it would be years before he actually assumed the throne. So while Saul continued to wear the royal robes, David roamed the hills around Bethlehem, seeking to know the King of kings. David's shepherding years provided the solitude—quiet times with God—necessary for him to write songs of praise and petition, to grow more expressive about his God's greatness, and to be humbled by his own humanity.

Ironically the battle for sanity inside Saul's mind could only be quieted by the soothing harp of none other than young David. Unaware that David had been anointed the next king, Saul invited him to live in the palace and be part of the king's court.

Reflection: While Saul was growing more self-absorbed and distant from God, David was growing closer to the heart of the Shepherd God of Israel. As David's sheep pastured in meadows and rested by still waters, his faith was shaped. His aloneness provided the hours of uninterrupted silence needed to hear the voice of God. These times with God provided confidence in God's presence and an unshakable foundation for his calling as king.

Our world fights solitude. We are more prone to amuse ourselves than to muse on the questions deep within us—and even less so to muse about the wonder, the majesty, and the adventure of life lived close to the Creator of the universe. Solitude and silence aren't options, but necessities, for closeness to the heart of God.

[The LORD] chose David to be
   his servant
  and took him from the sheep
   pens.
He brought him from tending the
   sheep
  so he could lead the flock, the
   people of Jacob,
  his own people, the people of
   Israel.
And David led them with an
   innocent heart
  and guided them with skillful
   hands.

PSALM 78:70–72

Preparing the new king

The Philistines had been a primary enemy of Israel for years. They controlled all the iron ore of the region and were well equipped with chariots of iron, protective armor, and a select core of fighting men who stood three feet taller than the average soldier. During Saul's reign the independent Philistine states united to forge a final victory over his forces, and an intimidating, nine-foot warrior named Goliath stood as their first line of attack. No one, including Saul, dared to confront the giant.

When David arrived at the standoff, he was outraged that this godless man, regardless of his size, would be allowed to terrorize and belittle the army of God. Armed with a slingshot and an undaunted faith in God, the teenage shepherd boy confidently approached his gigantic foe. While the Philistine hurled threats and ridiculed his opponent, the youngster knocked him to the ground with a stone. David killed the Philistine, but God won the battle.

From that day forward, David fought for God and soon became the most famous warrior in the land. As David's reputation grew, so did Saul's jealousy, until Saul tried to have him killed. But the king's own son Jonathan protected and befriended David. In fact, David and Jonathan became covenant friends, closer than brothers. Jonathan walked a fine line, being devoted to his father, while remaining loyal to David.

During one of his fits of rage, Saul suddenly threw his royal spear at David, but David's quick reflexes allowed him to dodge it. The bewildered

David ran to Samuel's home, and Samuel hustled him off to a town filled with prophets. Saul found out and sent soldiers to capture David, but when they arrived, God's Spirit was so strong that they could do nothing except worship God. Saul sent other soldiers, but the same thing happened again. Finally, Saul himself came, and he also fell on the ground, praising God. While Saul was on his face before God, David escaped.

Months later, during a massive battle with the Philistines, both Saul and Jonathan died. David mourned their deaths and honored them in song.

The stage was now set for David to become king.

Reflection: David led Israel's armies to great victories, and then had to run for his life and hide out in caves. He was anointed the future king of Israel, and then was almost killed at the hands of the present king. In the midst of his turmoil David could find refuge and constancy only in his God. Out of these times came many of the psalms we appreciate today. In the midst of our turbulent times — times of despair, fear, betrayal, grief — they point us to the ever-present and compassionate God who continues to protect, listen, rescue, guide, help, and encourage.

The LORD is my light and the one
  who saves me.
  I fear no one.
The LORD protects my life;
  I am afraid of no one.
Evil people may try to destroy my
  body.
  My enemies and those who
    hate me attack me,
but they are overwhelmed and
    defeated.
If an army surrounds me,
  I will not be afraid.
If war breaks out,
  I will trust the LORD....
During danger he will keep me
  safe in his shelter.
  He will hide me in his Holy
    Tent,
  or he will keep me safe on a
    high mountain....

LORD, hear me when I call;
  have mercy and answer me.
My heart said of you, "Go, worship him."
  So I come to worship you,
    LORD....
If my father and mother leave me,
  the LORD will take me in.
LORD, teach me your ways,
  and guide me to do what is
    right
  because I have enemies....

I truly believe
  I will live to see the LORD's
    goodness.
Wait for the LORD's help.
  Be strong and brave,
  and wait for the LORD's help.

PSALM 27

God demands respect

After a bitter battle between the remnants of Saul's family in the north and David's forces in the south, the thirty-year-old shepherd-turned-warrior was crowned king of Israel. David's army entered the strongly fortified city of Jerusalem through its water system, easily defeating the inhabitants, and David made it his capital. For centuries Jerusalem would remain the political and religious center of Israel.

After two crushing defeats of the Philistines, David commanded that the Ark of God be brought to Jerusalem. What a spectacular event that was. David and thirty thousand men accompanied the return. Perhaps many had never seen this chest that symbolized the presence of the God of Israel. Certainly they had forgotten how to treat it. The Ark was so holy that not even the priests were allowed to touch it but were to carry it on special poles. In this procession, however, God's Ark was placed on a cart pulled by oxen. When the oxen stumbled, Uzzah attempted to steady the Ark and died.

A few months later the priests attempted to move the Ark once again, this time carefully following God's guidelines. David and his singers led the Ark into Jerusalem with a procession of joyous dancing and singing and praising God.

With David as king, God expanded the borders of Israel east and west of the Jordan, as far north as the headwaters of the Euphrates, and as far south as the Gulf of Aqaba. God gave David great victories, and David gave God the credit.

Reflection: From our human vantage point, murder, rape, terrorism, and child abuse top the list of heinous sins. We understand the pain they cause, and we demand justice, preferably swift justice.

Sin, however, is first and foremost against God, not us. God makes it clear that treating that which is holy as if it were common is a grievous sin, whether it is touching the Ark or using God's name irreverently. Have we forgotten just how serious God is about that which is holy? Do we reach out without fear to touch the Ark?

When they came to the threshing floor of Nacon, Uzzah reached out and took hold of the ark of God, because the oxen stumbled. The LORD's anger burned against Uzzah because of his irreverent act; therefore God struck him down and he died there beside the ark of God.

2 SAMUEL 6:6–7, NIV

Praise the LORD!

I will thank the LORD with all my
    heart
    in the meeting of his good people.
The LORD does great things;
    those who enjoy them seek
    them.
What he does is glorious and
    splendid,
    and his goodness continues for-
    ever.
His miracles are unforgettable.
    The LORD is kind and merci-
    ful....

He sets his people free.
    He made his agreement ever-
    lasting.
    He is holy and wonderful.

Wisdom begins with respect for
    the LORD;
    those who obey his orders have
    good understanding.
    He should be praised forever.

PSALM 111

God disciplines his king

It was in the springtime when David—the king God chose as a man after his own heart—let his sexual passion overpower his moral compass. David slept with Bathsheba, the wife of Uriah, one of his best soldiers. When Bathsheba discovered she was pregnant, David tried to cover his sin and avoid scandal. After nothing else worked, he ultimately arranged for Uriah to die in battle. David then took Bathsheba into the palace and made her his wife. David had concealed his sin, but not from God.

The prophet Nathan confronted David, and in a remarkable example of remorse, David repented and confessed his sin against God. Although God forgave him and continued to love him, he didn't spare David the consequences of his sin, which would affect his family the rest of his life. This child of David and Bathsheba died within a week. Later, three of David's sons would die violently. One of them—Absalom—killed his older brother, rebelled against his father, and tried to usurp the throne. To keep from fighting his own son, David retreated from Jerusalem and lived east of the Jordan. In the power-hungry son's final battle with his father's soldiers, Absalom's forces were scattered, and while Absalom was riding through the woods trying to escape, his hair got caught in the branches of an oak tree and he died there.

Although David was far from a perfect king, during his reign the kingdom prospered, its enemies were defeated and its borders extended. God had promised David that his family and his kingdom would continue forever. His reign became a standard by which later kings would be judged. When David was old and about to die, he appointed his son Solomon to be king after him and charged him to be faithful to his God. Shortly afterward, the singer of Israel, the shepherd of Bethlehem, the warrior king, the man after God's own heart, died, and all of Israel mourned.

Reflection: One of the most amazing characteristics of God is his desire to restore our relationship with him through brokenness. When one of his own returns to him broken in spirit, God forgives and repairs, often making his child stronger than before. And in repentance comes a deeper relationship with the Father, possibly closer than at any other time in our lives.

God, be merciful to me
because you are loving.
Because you are always ready to
be merciful,
wipe out all my wrongs.
Wash away all my guilt
and make me clean again.

I know about my wrongs,
and I can't forget my sin.
You are the only one I have
sinned against;
I have done what you say is
wrong.
You are right when you speak
and fair when you judge....

You are not pleased by sacrifices,
or I would give them.
You don't want burnt offerings.
The sacrifice God wants is a
broken spirit.
God, you will not reject a heart
that is broken and sorry for
sin.

PSALM 51:1–17

Solomon rejects God's wisdom

Early in his reign, Solomon followed in the steps of his father, David, and sought help from God. He took the leaders of Israel to Gibeon, to the tabernacle, and offered a thousand sacrifices to God. When Solomon fell asleep that night, God appeared to him and asked what he wanted God to give him. Young and inexperienced, Solomon asked for what he felt he needed most—wisdom. God was so pleased with this request that he granted him wisdom beyond that of any other man, and fame and fortune as well.

Solomon reigned in peace and prosperity throughout his life. He was a writer, a poet, a political strategist, and a skillful businessman. He built a magnificent temple for God and joined the people in a massive dedication ceremony—blessing the people, leading a prayer of consecration, and offering sacrifices to God.

For himself and his seven hundred wives, Solomon built a palace that was even larger than the temple. To build these massive structures, he taxed the people heavily and forced them to work for the state. By the end of his reign the people lived in poverty while their king and his wives enjoyed great luxury.

To keep his many foreign wives happy, Solomon also built elaborate temples to strange gods and began to worship the idols himself. Although Solomon had a strong heritage, unparalleled wisdom direct from the hand of God, and all the worldly wealth a heart could desire, he lost his way and his devotion to God. And God became angry with Solomon.

God told Solomon he would tear the kingdom away from him and give it to one of his officers. But faithful to his promise to David, God would leave a portion of the kingdom in the hands of David's descendants. One tribe, the tribe of Judah, would be left for Solomon's son to rule.

Reflection: Solomon's wisdom was an endowment from God for the benefit of God's people. But Solomon's respect for and dependence upon God dwindled as the scope of his kingdom expanded. Eventually God had been replaced in the king's heart.

Solomon's drift away from God flashes like a giant warning light for us. God's blessings are not given to feed our pride; they are resources to share. If we abide by that principle, God will take care of our needs, and he will remain on the throne of our hearts.

Trust the LORD with all your heart,
and don't depend on your own
understanding.
Remember the LORD in all you
do,
and he will give you success.

Don't depend on your own wisdom.
Respect the LORD and refuse to
do wrong.
Then your body will be healthy,
and your bones will be strong.

Honor the LORD with your wealth
and the firstfruits from all your
crops.
Then your barns will be full,
and your wine barrels will
overflow with new wine.

Whenever you are able,
do good to people who need
help.

PROVERBS 3:5–10, 27

God shows himself to be God

When Solomon died, his son Rehoboam succeeded him, but the nation of Israel was torn in two. Rejecting Rehoboam's heavy hand on them, ten tribes set up a new kingdom in the north, under the rule of Jeroboam. Lest the people go back to Judah to worship at the temple in Jerusalem, Jeroboam set up two golden calves and revised history, claiming these idols represented the god that had brought their ancestors out of Egypt. To strengthen the separate identity of his kingdom and maintain his place as its king, he established a copy of Israel's religion, complete with feasts, holy days, and altars.

Over the next several decades, the northern kingdom experienced a succession of assassinations and insurrections, and their own civil war, before a dominant leader named Omri emerged. Omri built Samaria and made it his capital, but Omri and his son Ahab did more evil than any of the kings before them, leading the people farther and farther away from the holy God of Israel.

Enter Elijah. This dedicated, outspoken prophet of God constantly confronted Ahab and his Baal-worshiping wife, Jezebel. Elijah challenged Ahab to bring the prophets of Baal and Asherah to Mount Carmel for a "contest" with the God of Israel. Ahab accepted, and 850 prophets of Jezebel's false gods stood against Elijah, the prophet of God.

Elijah explained that each side was to build an altar and place a sacrifice on the altar, but the fire was to be provided by the god. Whichever god sent down fire would show himself as the true God. Jezebel's prophets went first. They prepared the sacrifice and spent all morning praying, dancing around the altar, and crying loudly to Baal, but nothing happened. Elijah began to taunt them, asking if Baal were asleep, or on a trip, or too busy to answer. All afternoon the prophets prayed even louder and cut themselves, but there was no answer.

Just before evening Elijah called the crowd closer. Then he rebuilt the altar of God which was there, dug a ditch around it, placed wood upon the altar and the sacrifice upon the wood. Next he asked that water be poured over the altar—three times—so that water drenched the sacrifice and filled the ditch. Then Elijah prayed that God would show the people who was the only true God.

Immediately heavenly fire fell from the sky, burning up the sacrifice, the wood, the rocks, and even the water in the ditch. Nothing was left but smoke. Seeing this awesome display of power, the crowd joined Elijah in chasing Jezebel's prophets into the valley where Elijah killed them all. That day, the brook Kishon flowed red with

At the time of sacrifice, the prophet Elijah stepped forward and prayed: "O LORD, God of Abraham, Isaac and Israel, let it be known today that you are God in Israel and that I am your servant and have done all these things at your command. Answer me, O LORD, answer me, so these people will know that you, O LORD, are God, and that you are turning their hearts back again."

1 KINGS 18:36–37, NIV

"Can you compare me to anyone?
  No one is equal to me or like me.
Some people are rich with gold
  and weigh their silver on the
    scales.
They hire a goldsmith, and he makes
  it into a god.
  Then they bow down and worship
    it.
They put it on their shoulders and
  carry it.
  They set it in its place, and there it
    stands;
  it cannot move from its place.
People may yell at it, but it cannot
  answer.
  It cannot save them from their
    troubles.
"Remember this, and do not forget it!
  Think about these things, you who
    turn against God.
Remember what happened long ago.
  Remember that I am God, and
    there is no other God.
I am God, and there is no one like
  me."

ISAIAH 46:5–9

the blood of Jezebel's prophets, and the people gathered at Carmel were struck with fear and awe.

Reflection: God has no competition. He describes himself as a jealous god, and he will go to great lengths to bring his errant children back to him. He continually manifests his deity and his power so that those who seek him can have no doubt that he, and he alone, is God. Anyone or anything that supplants his rule as lord of our lives is as powerless to save us as was Baal.

The LORD says, "Whoever loves me, I will save.
    I will protect those who know me.
They will call to me, and I will answer them.
    I will be with them in trouble;
    I will rescue them and honor them.
I will give them a long, full life,
    and they will see how I can save."

PSALM 91:14–16

The whispers of God

When Ahab returned to Jezreel and told Jezebel what had happened on Mount Carmel, she flew into a rage and sent a messenger to Elijah, proclaiming him as dead as her prophets. Despite God's recent demonstrations of power, Elijah fled in fear and headed toward another mountain — Mount Sinai.

Here, long ago, God's voice had thundered as he spoke to Moses, and the people had trembled. This time Elijah heard God, but not in the sound of the wind, the power of an earthquake, or the crackling of the fire. On this day Elijah heard God whisper. The all-powerful God gently asked Elijah why he was hiding in a cave. Elijah answered that he was the last faithful voice for God and he was hiding from those who wanted to kill him also. God assured Elijah that there were seven thousand people in the northern kingdom who were still faithful to God, that he was still in control of the nations, and that he had work for Elijah to do.

After the encounter in the cave, Elijah began preparing a prophet named Elisha to take his place. One day while Elisha and Elijah were walking together, God sent a fiery chariot to pick up the prophet and to carry him home to heaven in a whirlwind. And Elisha inherited the position and power of his mentor.

Reflection: Down through history God has spoken to his people in many ways—through thunder, burning bushes, angelic messengers, prophets like Moses. Incredible as they are, it's almost more amazing that God reduces his power to fit in a whisper, as he did with Elijah.

You may hear a whisper while you're reading or praying or worshiping. It may come when you're driving or meditating or hiking. A question, a request, a challenge may tug at your heart. Listen for God's voice, and when he whispers to your soul, don't close your mind to the call.

The LORD's voice is heard over
    the sea.
  The glorious God thunders;
  the LORD thunders over the
    ocean.
The LORD's voice is powerful;
  the LORD's voice is majestic....
The LORD's voice makes the
    lightning flash....
The LORD's voice shakes the oaks
  and strips the leaves off the
    trees.
In his Temple everyone says,
  "Glory to God!"

PSALM 29:3–9

The LORD said, "Go out and stand on the mountain in the presence of the LORD, for the LORD is about to pass by."

Then a great and powerful wind tore the mountains apart and shattered the rocks before the LORD, but the LORD was not in the wind. After the wind there was an earthquake, but the LORD was not in the earthquake. After the earthquake came a fire, but the LORD was not in the fire. And after the fire came a gentle whisper.

1 KINGS 19:11–12, NIV

Idols of the heart

While Ahab's youngest son, Jehoram, was ruling the northern kingdom, Ben-hadad of Syria besieged its capital. He surrounded the city so long that the citizens of Samaria ran out of food and a donkey's head and dove's dung were selling for a high price. There was even talk of cannibalism. King Jehoram blamed Elisha and threatened to kill him, but Elisha prevented him by announcing the siege would be over in twenty-four hours.

That very evening four lepers, who were kept outside the city gates, decided to surrender to the Syrians, but when they arrived at the perimeter of the enemy camp, no soldiers could be found. The Lord had covered the camp with sounds of chariots and horses, panicking the Syrians, who abandoned their possessions and ran for their lives. The lepers brought the good news back to the city, and by the next morning the starving people of Samaria were gathering the food and goods the Syrians had left behind.

Shortly afterward Elisha anointed Jehu as the next king of the northern kingdom. Jehu eliminated all descendants of Ahab in a bloody coup. Then he announced a religious assembly at the temple of Baal to celebrate his accession to the throne. When the ceremony was underway, Jehu commanded his soldiers to massacre the Baal worshipers.

Although Jehu destroyed Baal worship in the kingdom, he was not careful to follow God's law. God still did not reign in the people's hearts.

Reflection: Looking back on all the powerful ways God provided for and rescued his people, we have a hard time understanding how quickly they could forget and become obstinate once again. Even when the outward symbols of idol worship were destroyed, their hearts lagged behind. The prophets constantly warned them of the inevitable discipline of a holy God whom they defied with their rebellion, their worship of false gods, and their self-rule.

In reality, however, although our "idols" are different, are our hearts any less stubborn and forgetful?

The LORD said to Jehu, "You have done well in obeying what I said was right. You have done to the family of Ahab as I wanted. Because of this, your descendants as far as your great-great-grandchildren will be kings of Israel." But Jehu was not careful to follow the teachings of the LORD, the God of Israel, with all his heart. He did not stop doing the same sins Jeroboam had done, by which he had led Israel to sin.

2 KINGS 10:30–31

"My people, listen. I am warning
  you.
  Israel, please listen to me!
You must not have foreign gods;
  you must not worship any false
  god.
I, the LORD, am your God,
  who brought you out of Egypt.
  Open your mouth and I will
  feed you.

"But my people did not listen to
  me;
  Israel did not want me.
So I let them go their stubborn
  way
  and follow their own advice.
I wish my people would listen to
  me;
  I wish Israel would live my way.
Then I would quickly defeat their
  enemies
  and turn my hand against their
  foes."

PSALM 81:8–14

The unrelenting love of God

For a time both the northern and southern kingdoms enjoyed increased trade and great wealth, but society was corrupt. Although the Israelites gave up their idols and returned to the God of their heritage, their worship of him was a sham. The nation recognized it was favored by God, but all the while it abused the privileges and ignored the responsibilities. In the midst of great luxury, the poor remained. The people's sacrifices were numerous but meaningless. Even their right actions weren't matched by right hearts.

During the rule of another man named Jeroboam, the prophet Amos reminded the people that God is not blind to or unconcerned about injustice. The prophet boldly condemned the greed and immorality of the people and their heartless treatment of the poor. He warned, God would not merely punish them as he had in the past, but he would virtually destroy them as a nation. Amos's prophecy was soon fulfilled as Assyria invaded the northern kingdom and carried it off into captivity,

Hosea, a prophet contemporary with Amos, also delivered God's warnings—and in a most dramatic and unusual way. God used Hosea's relationship with his unfaithful wife to symbolize God's relationship with unfaithful Israel. Just as Hosea took his wife back after she was unfaithful, God loved Israel and would take her back and forgive her, even after she rejected and dishonored him.

Reflection: God rescued and tutored and guided and healed his people like a devoted father. In return he asked that his children love and obey him—to honor him as father—but they failed on every count.

God loved Israel with an unrelenting love, as a husband loves his wife, forgiving her and taking her back even though she ran after others. He longed for the time he could lift her up and bring out the best in her, but she rejected him.

How could Israel turn away from such love? How could we?

"When I called the people of Israel,
   they went away from me.
They offered sacrifices to the Baals
   and burned incense to the idols.
It was I who taught Israel to walk,
   and I took them by the arms,
but they did not understand
   that I had healed them.
I led them with cords of human kindness,
   with ropes of love.
I lifted the yoke from their neck
   and bent down and fed them....

"Israel, how can I give you up?
   How can I give you away, Israel?...
My heart beats for you,
   and my love for you stirs up my pity.
I won't punish you in my anger,
   and I won't destroy Israel again.
I am God and not a human;
   I am the Holy One, and I am among you."

HOSEA 11:2–9

The reluctant messenger

God directed the prophet Jonah to go to the wicked Assyrians with a clear message of judgment, but Jonah didn't want to go. He didn't fear them or their rejection. He feared success! Assyria was an enemy, and Jonah suspected they might repent and that God would forgive them. Jonah didn't want to help save them. Thinking he could avoid delivering the message, Jonah tried to run away from God. But when Jonah found himself in the pit of a fish's stomach, in the pit of the sea, and near death, he repented and begged God to save him.

God did save Jonah, and Jonah finally arrived in Nineveh, the Assyrian capital, where he delivered God's warning. And just as Jonah had feared, the people repented. The king even decreed that the people were to repent and give up their evil ways so perhaps God would spare them. God was pleased and withheld his judgment. But despite his own rescue, Jonah grew angry when God spared the thousands of Ninevites who repented.

Their repentance didn't last longer than a generation, however. Decades later, the prophet Nahum once again announced God's judgment on Nineveh. Nahum praised God's patience, not as weakness but as strength, and he assured the Assyrians that the almighty God always punishes the guilty. When evil is punished and destroyed, God is glorified. They could not expect to ultimately escape the judgment for their sins.

Reflection: When Jonah was caught in the stomach of the fish, he was glad God was quick to listen and to forgive. But he didn't want God responding to his enemy Nineveh in the same way. Praise God that he is the God of every nation, that he is a just God, and that he treats us not as we deserve but with infinite love and mercy. Praise God that his response to our repentance is one of his most "unhumanlike" characteristics.

[Jonah said,] "When I was in danger,
  I called to the LORD,
  and he answered me.
I was about to die,
  so I cried to you,
  and you heard my voice.
You threw me into the sea,
  down, down into the deep sea.
The water was all around me,
  and your powerful waves
    flowed over me....
  I thought I was locked in this
    prison forever,
but you saved me from the pit of
    death,
  LORD my God.
"When my life had almost gone,
  I remembered the LORD.
I prayed to you,
  and you heard my prayers in
    your Holy Temple."

JONAH 2:2–7

When God saw what the people [of Nineveh] did, that they stopped doing evil, he changed his mind and did not do what he had warned. He did not punish them.

But this made Jonah very unhappy, and he became angry. He prayed to the LORD, "When I was still in my own country this is what I said would happen, and that is why I quickly ran away to Tarshish. I knew that you are a God who is kind and shows mercy. You don't become angry quickly, and you have great love. I knew you would choose not to cause harm."

JONAH 3:10–4:2

Hope remains

The quality of life in the northern kingdom had disintegrated badly. The Israelites had all but forgotten the God of their ancestors. From the beginning, the northern kingdom had not only worshiped the false gods of the Canaanites, but the people had changed the worship of God into rituals devoid of life and meaning—no different than the worship of idols.

Finally, after generations of unfaithfulness despite God's warnings, God followed through on his promised punishment and allowed Assyria to invade and conquer Israel. Without God's protection, Israel was no match for the mighty armies of Assyria. After the city of Samaria fell, the people were deported, and the Assyrian king replaced the Israelites with people of his own. The replacements mixed with the Israelite stragglers left behind and eventually became known as Samaritans.

The Israelites were scattered throughout the Assyrian empire where the language, the rituals, and the social structure were all different. As strangers in a foreign land, they began to miss the God of their heritage, and they remembered his promise to restore them once again.

Reflection: One of the truisms of human nature is that we tend to discount the value of something until we lose it. Not until God's people were scattered throughout the Assyrian empire did they truly turn their hearts back to God. Alienated from their homeland and their places of worship, they clung to the hope that God would remember them and someday gather them up and bring them home, as he had promised.

Regardless of the situation, for God's people there is always hope, and with our repentance there is always God's promise of restoration.

Israel says, "I will look to the
   LORD for help.
  I will wait for God to save me;
  my God will hear me.
Enemy, don't laugh at me.
  I have fallen, but I will get up
   again.
I sit in the shadow of trouble
   now,
  but the LORD will be a light for
  me.
I sinned against the LORD,
  so he was angry with me,
but he will defend my case in
   court.
  He will bring about what is
  right for me...."

There is no God like you.
  You forgive those who are
  guilty of sin;
you don't look at the sins of your
  people
who are left alive.
You will not stay angry forever,
  because you enjoy being kind.
You will have mercy on us again;
  you will conquer our sins.
You will throw away all our sins
  into the deepest part of the sea.

MICAH 7:7–9, 18–19

Southern kingdom struggles

In the southern kingdom the people of God faced similar problems to those in the north. During the reign of Rehoboam, the grandson of David, the people ignored the commands of God, and so God permitted Shishak, king of Egypt, to invade Jerusalem and ransack the temple. God, however, did not let Shishak destroy the people, because they submitted themselves to God once again.

Not until Rehoboam's grandson Asa reigned did the southern kingdom truly move back toward God. Asa destroyed the idols and the places of idol worship and commanded the people to follow the God of their ancestors. When the Ethiopians attacked, Asa turned to God for help, and God gave Asa the victory. As long as the nation followed God and continued to rid itself of idol worship, God blessed them. But late in Asa's reign, the northern kingdom placed sanctions on Asa's kingdom, and Asa sought foreign alliances to protect them rather than turning to God for help.

God sent a prophet to have a "woodshed" talk with his misguided king, but this time Asa didn't listen to the Lord. Instead, he imprisoned the prophet and treated some of his own people cruelly. As a result of Asa's disobedience, the nation suffered through wars for the rest of his reign. Even when Asa became seriously ill, he did not look to God for help. Asa had begun well, but he ended his life with his back turned to God.

Reflection: Asa's reign started with power and ended with a whimper. Even though he had experienced God's trustworthiness as an ally, in Asa's later years he chose instead to depend on his own schemes. Perhaps Asa believed he could handle things on his own. Perhaps he had grown proud of his accomplishments. After all he had brought revival to the land, and the nation was at peace. But as soon as Asa tried to save the nation and himself by his own power, he failed, and the nation ended up at war. Anytime we put our faith in human abilities over God, we are certain to have conflict—and ultimately to fail.

Then Asa and the people made a promise before the LORD, shouting with a loud voice and blowing trumpets and sheep's horns. All the people of Judah were happy about the promise, because they had promised with all their heart. They looked for God and found him. So the LORD gave them peace in all the country.

2 CHRONICLES 15:14–15

At that time Hanani the seer came to Asa king of Judah and said to him, "You depended on the king of Aram to help you and not on the LORD your God. So the king of Aram's army escaped from you. The Cushites and Libyans had a large and powerful army and many chariots and horsemen. But you depended on the LORD to help you, so he handed them over to you. The LORD searches all the earth for people who have given themselves completely to him. He wants to make them strong. Asa, you did a foolish thing, so from now on you will have wars."

2 CHRONICLES 16:7–9

Power in praise

Asa's son Jehoshaphat renewed the effort to stay faithful to God. Recognizing the people's need to know more about God and his commands, Jehoshaphat organized teachers to travel throughout Judah, telling the people about the God of Abraham, Isaac, and Jacob.

As the nation grew stronger and the people more united in their common faith, the kings around them became concerned and fearful. Three of the surrounding nations joined forces in a plan to destroy Judah in one crushing assault on Jerusalem.

When Jehoshaphat learned of the impending attack, he publicly turned to God, admitted their powerlessness against such forces, and prayed for God to protect his people. God honored his prayer and revealed his plan to fight the battle for Jerusalem himself.

The next day Jehoshaphat selected praise singers to march in front of a rather meager army, and while they sang "Thank the LORD, because his love continues forever," God turned what would have been a massive ambush of Judah into a day of confusion for the enemy. He tricked the attackers into turning on each other so that at day's end, not a single enemy was left alive. It took God's people three days to gather all the equipment and supplies left behind.

Jehoshaphat was a good king, but even though God was trusted in the palace and worshiped in the temple, the people did not allow him in their hearts. So after the king died, the people returned to worshiping false gods.

Reflection: To the frightened Israelites how strange it must have seemed—sending their warriors into battle led by the choir. It boldly testified to their faith in and dependence upon God. Marching beyond the city walls and lifting their hearts and their hands to God in praise focused everyone on God, not themselves. It set every compass in the same direction. This was not a concert or mere pageantry; this was a supernatural experience shared with the unseen, all-powerful Conqueror God.

Like God's people of old, when we praise God, we proclaim our trust in him and his trustworthiness. We approach him like little children running to their father with arms raised, asking to be lifted and carried by a willing and loving father. Despite our enemies, in his arms we place our security, our hope, and our lives.

Jehoshaphat's army went out into the Desert of Tekoa early in the morning. As they were starting out, Jehoshaphat stood and said, "Listen to me, people of Judah and Jerusalem. Have faith in the LORD your God, and you will stand strong. Have faith in his prophets, and you will succeed." Jehoshaphat listened to the people's advice. Then he chose men to be singers to the LORD, to praise him because he is holy and wonderful. As they marched in front of the army, they said,

"Thank the LORD,
   because his love continues
   forever."

As they began to sing and praise God, the LORD set ambushes for the people of Ammon, Moab, and Edom who had come to attack Judah. And they were defeated.

2 CHRONICLES 20:20–22

LORD our Lord,
   your name is the most wonderful name in all the earth!
   It brings you praise in heaven above.
You have taught children and babies
   to sing praises to you
   because of your enemies.
And so you silence your enemies
   and destroy those who try to get even.

PSALM 8:1–2

The call of Isaiah

Over the years various kings of the southern kingdom attempted to restore the people's allegiance to God, but they were only minimally successful. King Uzziah and his son Jotham at least kept God as the public, national God of the people. While the prophet Zechariah was alive, Uzziah leaned heavily on his advice, and as long as Uzziah trusted God, he was successful in everything he did. He stood strong against his enemies and undertook numerous building projects. A generation experienced relative peace and prosperity.

After he became powerful, however, Uzziah grew proud and was unfaithful to God. Ignoring God's commands, he went into the temple to offer sacrifices, a duty reserved for the priests. As a consequence of his arrogance, God struck him with leprosy, and he lived the rest of his life as an outcast. When he died, his son Jotham reigned, but more significantly a new prophet accepted the call of God. His name was Isaiah.

The future of the southern kingdom was in question, but a concerned Isaiah was ready. In a vision that transported him into the throne room of the King of kings, Isaiah was overwhelmed. Angels stood above the majestic King and proclaimed his holiness. The throne room shook with the sound of their cries. In the presence of the holy God, Isaiah felt unclean. He couldn't speak a word of praise, only words of despair about his own sins. Instead of sentencing the unholy Isaiah to death, the King sent his angels to purify him and call him to the task of preparing the people for the certain consequences of their unfaithfulness.

After that day, God's prophet had the ear of at least three of the southern kingdom's next kings. His visions foretold both punishment and restoration for the people. He told of the day when all nations would find peace at the doorstep of Israel and of a suffering servant of God who would be executed for the sins of all people, making it possible for everyone to know the almighty, holy God of glory.

But that day was a long way off.

Reflection: Nothing can remain hidden in the brilliant light of God's holiness. In God's presence we are incapable of ignoring or hiding our sins, even those buried deep within us; we can do nothing but confess them. In moments of confession we find ourselves arm in arm with God. Like Isaiah, we are amazed that instead of being punished as we deserve, God forgives our guilt, cleanses our sins, and prepares us for his service.

[Isaiah] said, "Oh no! I will be destroyed. I am not pure, and I live among people who are not pure, but I have seen the King, the LORD All-Powerful."

One of the heavenly creatures used a pair of tongs to take a hot coal from the altar. Then he flew to me with the hot coal in his hand. The creature touched my mouth with the hot coal and said, "Look, your guilt is taken away, because this hot coal has touched your lips. Your sin is taken away."

Then I heard the Lord's voice, saying, "Whom can I send? Who will go for us?"

So I said, "Here I am. Send me!"

Then the Lord said, "Go and tell this to the people...."

ISAIAH 6:5–9

Happy is the person
    whose sins are forgiven,
    whose wrongs are pardoned.
Happy is the person
    whom the LORD does not consider
        guilty
    and in whom there is nothing false.

When I kept things to myself,
    I felt weak deep inside me.
    I moaned all day long.
Day and night you punished me.
    My strength was gone as in the
        summer heat.
Then I confessed my sins to you
    and didn't hide my guilt.
I said, "I will confess my sins to the
    LORD,"
    and you forgave my guilt.

PSALM 32:1–5

Hezekiah's restoration

Jotham's son Ahaz reigned over the southern kingdom after him, but he followed in the evil ways of the Canaanite nations. Ahaz closed the doors of the temple and placed altars to false gods on every street corner in Jerusalem and in every city in Judah. He even sacrificed his own sons to the false gods. On his death, he was not buried with the other kings, because of his wickedness, and his son Hezekiah took his place.

Hezekiah's first command was to reopen the temple doors and to cleanse the temple. When the temple was cleansed, sacrifices were offered, the people sang, and the priests played David's instruments. On that day, Hezekiah and the people knelt and praised God and dedicated themselves and the temple to his service once again. Hezekiah then sent messengers throughout Israel, inviting the people to come to Jerusalem to celebrate the Passover. God's people responded to Hezekiah's lead so that the Passover celebration was greater than anything in all Israel since Solomon was king. In fact, the people extended the celebration for seven extra days. These were exciting times of worship and praise.

Fourteen years later Sennacherib of Assyria surrounded Jerusalem and proclaimed loudly that no God could protect Jerusalem from the hands of the mighty king of Assyria. In common terms, he dared God to do something. Hezekiah prayed to God for help, and Isaiah provided God's answer. That night God defended his honor and his people, and 185,000 Assyrian soldiers died. Disgraced and defeated, Sennacherib returned to his home and shortly afterward was killed by his own sons.

Reflection: God will always defend his honor. When his children worship him and obey him and remember his relationship with their ancestors, he is honored. When evil actions are thwarted and human pride is broken, he is honored. Even in the discipline of his disobedient children, he is honored. Ultimately, God will be honored — through us, or in spite of us.

God, the Holy One, says, "Can you
    compare me to anyone?
    Is anyone equal to me?"
Look up to the skies.
    Who created all these stars?
He leads out the army of heaven one
    by one
    and calls all the stars by name.
Because he is strong and powerful,
    not one of them is missing.

People of Jacob, why do you com-
    plain?
    People of Israel, why do you say,
"The LORD does not see what hap-
    pens to me;
    he does not care if I am treated
    fairly"?
Surely you know.
    Surely you have heard.
The Lord is the God who lives forever,
    who created all the world....
    No one can understand how
    great his wisdom is.
He gives strength to those who are
    tired
    and more power to those who
    are weak.
Even children become tired and need
    to rest,
    and young people trip and fall.
But the people who trust the LORD
    will become strong again.
They will rise up as an eagle in the
    sky;
    they will run and not need rest;
    they will walk and not become
    tired.

ISAIAH 40:25–31

The God of second chances

While that great victory was still fresh in his memory, Hezekiah became seriously ill, and Isaiah told him to get his affairs in order. But the king begged God for more years of life, and moved by Hezekiah's tears, the compassionate God of life granted him fifteen more years. During those years Hezekiah became wealthy and famous, and God tested him to see what was in his heart. Although Hezekiah accomplished many great tasks, his pride in what he possessed hurt his relationship with God. Isaiah warned him that eventually the southern kingdom—and even his family—would be carried off to Babylon.

When Hezekiah died, his son Manasseh reigned after him and chose to act against God's clear instructions, leading Judah closer to destruction. He rebuilt the shrines to false gods, introduced more Assyrian gods, revived child sacrifices, and filled Jerusalem's streets with the blood of innocent people. Manasseh would not listen to God's warnings, so God sent the Assyrians to capture him and imprison him in Babylon.

Imprisoned, alone, and powerless, he found humility and a spirit of repentance. God heard his prayer and forgave him and made it possible for Manasseh to return to Jerusalem. There he spent the last years of his reign, ridding the nation of the altars to false gods he had encouraged before, but he couldn't rid the people of the influence of the past years.

Reflection: The compassionate King of kings granted Hezekiah's request and blessed him with more years, but during those years Hezekiah grew proud and distant from the Giver of life. On the other hand, our listening, forgiving God heard Manasseh's prayers for mercy and granted him a second chance as king. Clearly our God is a God who listens and responds to our pleas. He is the God of second chances.

As Manasseh suffered, he begged the LORD his God for help and humbled himself before the God of his ancestors. When Manasseh prayed, the LORD heard him and had pity on him. So the LORD let him return to Jerusalem and to his kingdom. Then Manasseh knew that the LORD is the true God.

2 CHRONICLES 33:12–13

Praise the LORD, all you who respect him.
All you descendants of Jacob, honor him;
fear him, all you Israelites.
He does not ignore those in trouble.
He doesn't hide from them
but listens when they call out to him.

PSALM 22:23–24

Revival in the land

Manasseh may have repented, but his son Amon didn't. He ruled in the same way his unconverted father had, until he was assassinated and his eight-year-old son, Josiah, became king. At sixteen, Josiah began a personal search for the God of David, and within a few years, he began destroying the false gods and shrines introduced by his father and grandfather. He smashed the altars and ground the idols into dust. Then he began restoring the temple of the true God.

In the process, the high priest discovered an old scroll containing the laws of God. When Josiah read the scroll to see what the God of Moses required of his people, Josiah was devastated. Now he knew why his kingdom had not been blessed by God, and he knew what they must do, even if it was too late to avoid God's judgment.

Josiah pledged his allegiance to the God of his forefathers and asked the people of Jerusalem to do the same. Then he urged them to eliminate anything connected with idol worship, and he centralized the worship of God in Jerusalem. They celebrated the Passover as a national rededication to the faithful and merciful God. For the first time, revival was based on written authority—on the newly discovered Word of God.

While Josiah was king, Jeremiah was called to be God's prophet. His message was not one of reform and revival; it was one of impending devastation. The people of God could be fully restored and reconciled, but first they would be torn down and destroyed.

Reflection: How fortunate for the Israelites that they found the scrolls of God's law before the fall of Jerusalem and their exile to a strange country. With these written teachings fathers and mothers would be able to teach their children the commands of their holy God.

It's hard to imagine trying to know God without having access to his teachings, his Word. Although knowing God's teachings doesn't guarantee personal knowledge of the teacher, if we desire to know the teacher, we will seek to know his teachings. Throughout God's encounters with his people, we see this dual theme: We are to love God (to know him) and to obey him (to know his Word and follow it). Either alone is insufficient.

Happy are those who live pure
    lives,
    who follow the LORD's teachings.
Happy are those who keep his
    rules,
    who try to obey him with their
    whole heart.
They don't do what is wrong;
    they follow his ways.
LORD, you gave your orders
    to be obeyed completely.
I wish I were more loyal
    in obeying your demands.
Then I would not be ashamed
    when I study your commands.
When I learned that your laws
    are fair,
    I praised you with an honest
    heart.
I will obey your demands,
    so please don't ever leave me....

Open my eyes to see
    the miracles in your teachings....

Those who love your teachings
    will find true peace,
    and nothing will defeat them.

PSALM 119:1–8, 18, 165

121

The discipline of ~~God~~

Even during the reform of Josiah's reign, the people remained self-deceived and calloused. They refused to heed Jeremiah's words of warning. After all, they had recent memories of the greatest Passover feast in generations. Surely God would never allow his city and his temple to be destroyed. When King Josiah died, the people mourned deeply, but the revival died with him. And the judgment predicted by Jeremiah loomed on the horizon.

Another prophet at this time—Habakkuk—was filled with questions about the conditions he saw in Judah. How could a holy God continue to allow such wickedness in the land? Had God turned his back on his children? In response to Habakkuk's questions, God revealed his plan to use Babylon as his arm of punishment. Instead of that settling the issue, Habakkuk then wondered aloud how a holy God could use such an unholy nation for his purposes. After all, as unfaithful as God's people had been, surely they were better by far than the Babylonians. God assured Habakkuk that Babylon would also be punished, but what he required of his people was to trust God, no matter what the circumstances.

Stubborn King Zedekiah was ruling the southern kingdom when God permitted Nebuchadnezzar, king of Babylon, to capture and finally destroy Jerusalem, the temple, and the city walls. Because the people had been unfaithful and disloyal for so long, God allowed his city to be completely devastated and his people to be exiled to Babylon. For the Israelites the unthinkable had happened. The articles within the temple were confiscated and carried off to Babylon, and the temple and Jerusalem, the glorious city of David, were burned to the ground. The southern kingdom was gone.

Jeremiah, God's prophet of doom, lived through the destruction he had foretold. While the best and brightest people were hustled off to Babylon, he chose to stay in Judah with the poor people whom Nebuchadnezzar left behind.

Reflection: Our merciful God sees the long view. Unfaithful Israel had to be punished. But when they turned back to him, God would restore them in preparation for the coming Messiah who would introduce a new kingdom, a spiritual kingdom, that would expand out of Jerusalem and cover the earth.

God does some of his greatest work in the midst of his discipline. He doesn't ask us to understand it; he simply calls us to be faithful and trust his lead—and to wait quietly for his salvation.

LORD, remember my suffering
    and my misery,
    my sorrow and trouble.
Please remember me
    and think about me.
But I have hope
    when I think of this:

The LORD's love never ends;
    his mercies never stop.
They are new every morning;
    LORD, your loyalty is great.
I say to myself, "The LORD is
    mine,
    so I hope in him."
The LORD is good to those who
    hope in him,
    to those who seek him.
It is good to wait quietly
    for the LORD to save....

The Lord will not reject
    his people forever.
Although he brings sorrow,
    he also has mercy and great
    love.
He does not like to punish people
    or make them sad.

LAMENTATIONS 3:19–33

God's plan for new life

In Babylon the people had no king, no temple, no city of their own, and no land. All they had was God. Yet King Nebuchadnezzar treated them with unexpected dignity. He gave them fields and homes and permitted them to own businesses. A few even became trusted advisers to the king. The people of God, now called Jews, resided in the greatest city of their day, but their hearts were back in Jerusalem.

The prophet Ezekiel helped keep their memories of Jerusalem alive. God gave him graphic visions with unmistakable messages. In one such vision Ezekiel stood at the edge of a valley full of dry bones. God told Ezekiel to prophesy to the bones and tell them to come to life. When Ezekiel gave the command, the rattle of bones snapping together echoed across the valley. God put flesh and skin on the skeletons, and before long a mighty army stood before the amazed prophet.

God used this incredible experience to demonstrate the power of his redeeming love. Even though the nation of Israel was as dead as the bones, God would soon bring his beloved people back to life. They would again live in the homeland. They would again have an identity as a nation. Because of God's undying love, he would soon raise his people out of the ashes of exile into a new life.

Reflection: Our God is perfectly capable of invading our world with the impossible. In the beginning he created life with his words and his breath. He surely could create new life with the bones of past life. God does not merely reclaim his people; he resurrects them, giving them new life and a new identity. In our limited understanding we are pleased with reclaiming the best of what we've already experienced. God, on the other hand, always plans for more than we are capable of anticipating.

"This is what the Lord GOD says: I am going to take the people of Israel from among the nations where they have gone. I will gather them from all around and bring them into their own land. I will make them one nation in the land, on the mountains of Israel. One king will rule all of them. They will never again be two nations; they will not be divided into two kingdoms anymore. They will not continue to make themselves unclean by their idols, their statues of gods which I hate, or by their sins. I will save them from all the ways they sin and turn against me, and I will make them clean. Then they will be my people, and I will be their God."

EZEKIEL 37:21–23

God's new kingdom foretold

One night King Nebuchadnezzar had a dream that bothered him greatly. He asked his fortunetellers and magicians to tell him both the dream and its meaning. His request was an impossible one, they responded. No man could do what the king asked.

God, the source of Nebuchadnezzar's dream, revealed the dream and its meaning to Daniel, a bright and devoted young Israelite who had become an adviser to the king. After giving God the credit, Daniel described the massive image the king had seen: The head was gold, the chest and arms were silver, its torso and thighs were bronze, its legs were iron, and its feet were a mixture of iron and clay. Then Daniel told of the mysterious rock that struck the image, destroying it and continuing until it became a mountain that filled the earth.

Daniel then told Nebuchadnezzar God's message. The almighty God of Israel, the God who gives all kings power and authority, had given Nebuchadnezzar—the head of gold—the right to rule. Other kingdoms would come after Nebuchadnezzar's, but none would be as great as his until God set up his own kingdom. Then God's kingdom would crush all who challenged it, and it would never be destroyed.

Nothing would stop God's coming kingdom.

Reflection: The mysterious dream of Nebuchadnezzar brought God's message of hope for Israel. Although three other world powers would follow Babylon (Persia, Greece, and Rome), God himself would then carve out his own new kingdom, and that kingdom would be the greatest of all.

God was planning to redefine the concept of kingdom. His kingdom would not come and go like all earthbound empires; the all-powerful ruler of heaven and earth has a kingdom that lasts forever and will never be overthrown.

Daniel said:
"Praise God forever and ever,
  because he has wisdom and
    power.
He changes the times and seasons
    of the year.
  He takes away the power of
    kings
  and gives their power to new
    kings.
He gives wisdom to those who
    are wise
  and knowledge to those who
    understand.
He makes known secrets that are
    deep and hidden;
  he knows what is hidden in
    darkness,
  and light is all around him."

DANIEL 2:20–22

"The God of heaven will set up another kingdom that will never be destroyed or given to another group of people. This kingdom will crush all the other kingdoms and bring them to an end, but it will continue forever."

DANIEL 2:44

Testing commitment

After Daniel successfully interpreted Nebuchadnezzar's dream, Nebuchadnezzar gave him a high position in the country. At Daniel's request, Nebuchadnezzar also appointed Daniel's friends Shadrach, Meshach, and Abednego as leaders over Babylon.

Although Nebuchadnezzar had seen the power and greatness of Daniel's God, he made a gold statue ninety feet high and commanded everyone under his authority to bow down and worship it. Shadrach, Meshach, and Abednego refused. The king was so angry at their disobedience that he commanded they be thrown into a blazing furnace. Confident that if God wanted to save them from the fire he would, Shadrach, Meshach, and Abednego trusted God's will for their lives more than they feared the fire. God rewarded their faith and devotion by shielding them from the flames; they weren't even scorched. The king was so astonished by the power of the Israelite God that he commanded anyone who spoke against the God of Shadrach, Meshach, and Abednego to be killed.

Through the years and succeeding kings of Babylon, Daniel remained an important leader in Babylon and a man of faith and integrity. Three times a day he prayed to God. But a new king, Darius, instituted a law forbidding the people to pray to any god except the king, under penalty of being tossed to the lions. Daniel refused and was thrown in with the lions, but Daniel's ever-present God shut the mouths of the lions and protected him. Like his predecessor, Nebuchadnezzar, Darius issued a decree that everyone in his kingdom should respect the God of Daniel. Even in this foreign land God was at work, demonstrating his power and his faithfulness to those who trusted him.

As he had done in the wilderness time, God used the exile as a period of preparation for his people. If the Jews would trust him and wait for him to work his plan, they would see him as a loving, forgiving, and protective Father who was eager to reveal his great plans for his children everywhere.

Reflection: Like a proud father, God loves it when we obey him, when we trust him to keep his promises, when we put our very lives in his hands. When we choose to reflect his character—whether anyone's looking—God is glorified in heaven and on earth.

Nebuchadnezzar said, "Shadrach, Meshach, and Abednego,…if you bow down and worship the statue I made, that will be good. But if you do not worship it, you will immediately be thrown into the blazing furnace. What god will be able to save you from my power then?"

Shadrach, Meshach, and Abednego answered the king, saying, "Nebuchadnezzar, we do not need to defend ourselves to you. If you throw us into the blazing furnace, the God we serve is able to save us from the furnace. He will save us from your power, O king. But even if God does not save us, we want you, O king, to know this: We will not serve your gods or worship the gold statue you have set up."

DANIEL 3:14–18

Then King Darius wrote a letter to all people and all nations, to those who spoke every language in the world:…

I am making a new law for people in every part of my kingdom. All of you must fear and respect the God of Daniel.

Daniel's God is the living God;
    he lives forever.
His kingdom will never be destroyed,
    and his rule will never end.
God rescues and saves people
    and does mighty miracles
    in heaven and on earth.
He is the one who saved Daniel
    from the power of the lions.

DANIEL 6:25–27

Israel returns

When the Babylonian kings invaded a nation, they deported the conquered people. But when Cyrus of Persia captured Babylon, he permitted the conquered people to return to their own lands. Just as Jeremiah had foretold, the Jews were permitted to return to their homeland. God not only provided for his people to leave; they were commissioned to return and were given the protection and resources needed to rebuild their nation.

The first group to leave was led by Zerubbabel. These eager Jews rebuilt the altar and began work on the temple foundation before they became distracted and discouraged. It took the urging of a prophet named Haggai to rekindle the people's efforts. This time idols weren't the main culprit. Life was hard, food and clothes were in short supply, and prices were soaring because the people had their priorities twisted. Everyone was wrapped up in his own concerns with little thought for God. Haggai pricked the nation's conscience, and work began again.

The second group of settlers came with Ezra, a "teaching" priest. Along with restoring the nation and the temple, the people set out to restore their relationship with the God of their heritage. Ezra and the priests collected the sacred writings that had been handed down through the years. They not only gathered and copied these writings, they scheduled regular times to read the scrolls aloud and to explain them to the people. The people stood for hours, listening to the words of God, and as they understood God's message to them, they wept and worshiped and celebrated.

Ezra set the wheels in motion to assure their faithfulness to the forgiving God of their heritage. The goal was to develop a nation of people as faithful as Abraham, as obedient as Moses, and as close to the heart of God as David.

Reflection: What a portrayal of the power of God's Word. When the people heard God's message and had it explained to them, they stood for hours and listened carefully, they praised the Lord with upraised arms, they fell on their faces and worshiped him, they wept, they shared their food with others, and they ultimately rejoiced in the God of the Word.

With our accessibility to the Bible, if only we could capture even a part of their pure respect and awe for God's Word.

At the square by the Water Gate Ezra read the Teachings out loud from early morning until noon to the men, women, and everyone who could listen and understand. All the people listened carefully to the Book of the Teachings....

Ezra opened the book in full view of everyone, because he was above them. As he opened it, all the people stood up. Ezra praised the LORD, the great God, and all the people held up their hands and said, "Amen! Amen!" Then they bowed down and worshiped the LORD with their faces to the ground.

These Levites explained the Teachings to the people as they stood there....

Then Nehemiah the governor, Ezra the priest and teacher, and the Levites who were teaching said to all the people, "This is a holy day to the LORD your God. Don't be sad or cry." All the people had been crying as they listened to the words of the Teachings....

Then all the people went away to eat and drink, to send some of their food to others, and to celebrate with great joy. They finally understood what they had been taught.

NEHEMIAH 8:3–12

Rebuilding the wall

Almost a century after Zerubbabel led the first group back to the homeland, the Jews in Jerusalem were still discouraged and weak. Something was missing. There was no sense of identity and no security against their enemies. When Nehemiah, who was still in Babylon, heard of the miserable conditions in Jerusalem, he cried, fasted, and prayed, and God honored his prayers. King Artaxerxes not only sent Nehemiah to Jerusalem with a commission to rebuild it, but Artaxerxes provided him with army officers and letters to guarantee his safe passage.

Upon his arrival Nehemiah secretly surveyed the condition of the wall. Then he met with local leaders and the priests to tell them the reason for his coming. Nehemiah wanted to restore Jerusalem, beginning with the reconstruction of the walls around the city. The leaders and priests agreed, and the work began with everyone contributing wholeheartedly.

Despite ridicule and threats from the leaders of surrounding regions, the work went well until the wall was completed to half its intended height. Then the enemies of the Israelites threatened war. Nehemiah and the people prayed and scheduled guards on the wall both day and night. In less than two months the wall was completed. There was no doubt, even in the minds of their enemies, that God had protected them and granted them success.

As long as Nehemiah was governor of Jerusalem, he took care of the poor and encouraged the people to follow the Lord, but something was still missing. When Nehemiah returned to Babylon, the people once again ignored God's commands. The prophet Malachi reminded the people that

God still loved them but that he would also judge them for their wickedness. The closing promise of Malachi pictures the time when the heavenly Father would send his prophet "Elijah" to change the hearts of his creation, to turn the hearts of fathers toward their children and children toward their fathers. That's what had been missing—changed hearts.

Reflection: It's easy to get discouraged when God doesn't respond to our beck and call, when things don't happen as we think they should, or when life seems unfair. When we struggle with discouragement, it usually means we have let our focus slip from God to ourselves. But if we turn our hearts toward his fatherhood, his unquestionable and unending care for his children, then our courage and hope grow—despite our circumstances.

The LORD says, "You have said terrible things about me.

"But you ask, 'What have we said about you?'

"You have said, 'It is useless to serve God. It did no good to obey his laws and to show the LORD All-Powerful that we were sorry for what we did. So we say that proud people are happy. Evil people succeed. They challenge God and get away with it.'"

Then those who honored the LORD spoke with each other, and the LORD listened and heard them. The names of those who honored the LORD and respected him were written in his presence in a book to be remembered.

The LORD All-Powerful says, "They belong to me; on that day they will be my very own. As a parent shows mercy to his child who serves him, I will show mercy to my people. You will again see the difference between good and evil people, between those who serve God and those who don't."

MALACHI 3:13–18

Preparing for the Messiah

Generations passed after Malachi died, and the years brought many changes. The Philistines, Assyrians, and Babylonians were gone. Many Jews still lived in the promised land, but others were scattered throughout the known world. Nebuchadnezzar's dream had been fulfilled. The golden age of Greece, with Socrates, Plato, Aristotle, and Alexander the Great, had come and gone. Rome had become the dominant world power. In the midst of all the change God's people had but two things they could truly call their own: the scrolls containing God's Word and their persistent hope in the coming Messiah and his new kingdom.

Everyone had different opinions about this Messiah. Some saw him as a prophet who would bring revival and repentance to the land. Some expected a warrior king like David, who would defeat the Romans and make Israel great again. Others were looking for a Messiah who would introduce them to the new covenant and God's own Spirit. No one seemed to expect one man to be all of the above.

After all the years of anticipation, what a surprise it must have been the day the angel Gabriel announced the birth of a new prophet, a prophet who would prepare the people for the long-awaited Messiah. He foretold John's unprecedented power as a prophet and of his ministry of reuniting families and turning hearts toward God. Of all the prophets God had called, John the Baptist would be privileged to introduce the Son of God to the people of God.

John carried out his ministry in the countryside, the wilderness; there he preached God's message to the crowds who came out to hear him. His message was simple and powerful: repent—turn to God—and get ready for the new kingdom. He called for uncommon virtue and purity of motive, and his message was just the beginning.

Reflection: Throughout God's history with his people, the wilderness has played an important role. It offers few distractions and enough solitude for people to rethink their priorities and hear the call of God. Wilderness times can open our eyes to God's presence and our ears to his desires. John's wilderness call was exactly what God's people needed to hear—repent of your sins and prepare for the coming Messiah.

John's message is just as relevant for us. May we escape the noise of our daily lives long enough and often enough to hear that same message.

At this time, the word of God came to John son of Zechariah in the desert. He went all over the area around the Jordan River preaching a baptism of changed hearts and lives for the forgiveness of sins. As it is written in the book of Isaiah the prophet:

"This is a voice of one
  who calls out in the desert:
'Prepare the way for the Lord.
  Make the road straight for
    him....
And all people will know about
  the salvation of God!'"

LUKE 3:2–6

135

Immanuel announced

Six months after the angel Gabriel foretold the birth of the prophet John, Gabriel appeared again to announce another birth—the birth of the Messiah himself. This time Gabriel was sent to a teenage girl promised to be married to a carpenter named Joseph. She had been selected to be the mother of the Messiah while she was still a virgin. At first she was afraid, unsure. How could this happen?

The hope of the world hung there as young Mary pondered the unbelievable message from Gabriel. The God of heaven was moving ever closer to his people. His heavenly presence had been experienced on mountains, then in the tabernacle, and now his presence would be living in human form, inside the womb of a teenager. She had been handpicked by God to bring Immanuel into the world. After Gabriel calmed her fears, she was humbled by God's extraordinary blessing. How could she say no to Almighty God?

Mary's response was perfect: "I am the Lord's servant. Let this happen to me as you say!" No mother, before or after Mary, has had an experience that can compare to Mary's next nine months—feeling the Savior of the world, the Son of God, kicking in her womb.

Reflection: To the hosts of heaven and the legions of angels this must have seemed like a risky venture at best—to place the hope of the world in the response and hands of an unproven teenager. Yet God in his wisdom looks for those who, like Mary, willingly place their future in his hands and say, "I am the servant of the Lord. Let this happen to me as you say."

Then Mary said,
"My soul praises the Lord;
  my heart rejoices in God my
    Savior,
because he has shown his concern
    for his humble servant girl.
From now on, all people will say
    that I am blessed,
  because the Powerful One has
    done great things for me.
  His name is holy.
God will show his mercy forever
    and ever
  to those who worship and serve
    him.
He has done mighty deeds by his
    power.
  He has scattered the people
    who are proud
  and think great things about
    themselves.
He has brought down rulers from
    their thrones
  and raised up the humble.
He has filled the hungry with
    good things
  and sent the rich away with
    nothing.
He has helped his servant, the
    people of Israel,
  remembering to show them
    mercy
as he promised to our ancestors,
  to Abraham and to his children
    forever."

LUKE 1:46–55

137

God becomes flesh

Mary and Joseph were in Bethlehem when Jesus was born. Due to crowded conditions in the town, they were forced to stay in a stable. In fact, Jesus spent his first night in human form sleeping in a hay-filled feed trough. While God was getting used to breathing on his own and learning to cry, Bethlehem slept. The Son of the Almighty was now wrapped in human skin—fragile, hungry, dependent; the Father had placed his only Son in the loving care of a young novice mother, living among everyday folks.

The people of Bethlehem were unaware that the Savior of the world, the Messiah, the Christ, the Prince of Peace, the Son of God, was sleeping in an ordinary stable just up the street and around the corner. They didn't hear the angels bursting forth in song, announcing his birth. They weren't looking for a star leading heaven and earth to the back alleys of Bethlehem.

But the shepherds were awake, tending their sheep, possibly on the very hillsides David roamed with his flocks centuries before. Suddenly the shepherds were surrounded by dazzling brightness as an angel brought the announcement that had been anticipated for centuries. These nameless men were the first to hear God's incredible news—the birth of the Messiah.

God had opened the windows of heaven, and for a moment the shepherds could see the glory of the Lord and hear the praises of the angels. Jesus had traded his home in the presence of God for the loving arms of an ordinary couple, from an ordinary town, in an ordinary corner of the world.

Reflection: Jesus voluntarily left the glory of heaven for the vulnerable, helpless confines of a newborn human body. He came to earth, not with the demands of a tyrant king, but as a gift. As Mary rejoiced, angels sang, and shepherds marveled, God presented the divine to humanity in a form it could understand—its own frail form.

Christ himself was like God in everything.
But he did not think that being equal with God was something to be used for his own benefit.
But he gave up his place with God and made himself nothing.
He was born to be a man and became like a servant.
And when he was living as a man, he humbled himself and was fully obedient to God, even when that caused his death—death on a cross.
So God raised him to the highest place.
God made his name greater than every other name
so that every knee will bow to the name of Jesus—
everyone in heaven, on earth, and under the earth.
And everyone will confess that Jesus Christ is Lord
and bring glory to God the Father.

PHILIPPIANS 2:6–11

The boy who would be king

This tiny baby, tucked away in Bethlehem, rocked the world from the moment he appeared. Angels filled heaven and earth with praises to him, shepherds left their flocks to see him, wise men traveled hundreds of miles to worship him, King Herod tried his best to kill him, and under God's direction Mary and Joseph fled in the middle of the night to protect him.

Yet we know very little about Jesus' early years. He probably grew up playing among the shavings of Joseph's carpenter's bench. He likely learned to read and write in the synagogue, along with the other boys in the neighborhood. Like other Jewish families, Jesus and Mary and Joseph celebrated the Jewish feast days.

The spring after his twelfth birthday Jesus accompanied his family to Jerusalem for the Passover Feast. Crowds filled the narrow streets and temple courts. Thousands of families gathered inside the colonnades. The outer court was more than two football fields long, so it was easy to get lost in the crowd.

After the feast, the boy who would be Savior slipped away from Mary and Joseph, but he wasn't lost. He found the temple teachers and spent hours talking with the priests and instructors. As a boy on the edge of manhood, he listened and questioned. The amazed temple teachers had no idea who he was, but he knew.

When his parents found him, Jesus was in a deep discussion with the teachers. Perhaps he was asking questions designed to help them accept the coming Messiah. Even as a young man, Jesus knew who his father was, and he was already bent on doing what his Father had sent him to do.

Reflection: The teachers missed their chance. They were sitting with the Messiah, looking into the face of the God who created their world and everything in it, and they didn't know it. Years later at least a few of them must have remembered the moment and regretted what they missed. How tragic for them—or for us—to be in the presence of God, to hear his words, to speak with him, and never recognize his presence.

So you should look for the LORD
before it is too late;
you should call to him while he
is near.
The wicked should stop doing
wrong,
and they should stop their evil
thoughts.
They should return to the LORD
so he may have mercy on them.
They should come to our God,
because he will freely forgive
them.

The LORD says, "My thoughts are
not like your thoughts.
Your ways are not like my
ways.
Just as the heavens are higher
than the earth,
so are my ways higher than
your ways
and my thoughts higher than
your thoughts.
Rain and snow fall from the sky
and don't return without water-
ing the ground.
They cause the plants to sprout
and grow,
making seeds for the farmer
and bread for the people.
The same thing is true of the
words I speak.
They will not return to me
empty.
They make the things happen that
I want to happen,
and they succeed in doing what
I send them to do."

ISAIAH 55:6–11

141

Facing desert temptations

Years later, when Jesus was a grown man, he left the shavings of carpentry and the confines of his home in Nazareth, and accepted his true identity—the mantle of Messiah, the Christ. As his first step in connecting with the sins of the people, he came to Bethany to be baptized by John.

When John and Jesus came up out of the Jordan River, God threw open the windows of heaven and boldly proclaimed his family relationship with this unique human. While Jesus was praying, God confirmed Jesus as his son—"This is my son." In a way the Father was introducing humankind to his one and only Son. Mary was Jesus' mother, but God was his true father. Second, God affirmed his love for Jesus—"whom I love." They were bonded together by divine love. Third, God revealed his delight in Jesus' life—"in whom I am well pleased." He wanted those around Jesus and those who came after Jesus to know that the God of heaven was pleased with the direction of his Son's life.

After his extraordinary baptism, Jesus retreated into the desert for forty days of fasting and solitude. His time alone must have helped him focus on the mission that lay before him. It also provided a good opportunity for Satan to test him. At the end of Jesus' forty days, when he was numbed by hunger, Satan came calling. The master deceiver had one simple goal—to get Jesus to alter his mission.

Three times Satan offered Jesus a different path. And three times Jesus refused, quoting his Father's words.

The first was an appeal to Jesus' human needs. After all, the Son of God could surely turn stones into bread to satisfy his hunger. But Jesus refused to use his supernatural power to please himself. He chose, instead, to trust the care of his father.

For the second test, Satan took Jesus to the top of the temple in Jerusalem and dared him to jump. If Jesus would jump, God would rescue him, the people would be dazzled, and Jesus would be famous and popular. Satan must have realized that Jesus didn't come to win the people by mere theatrics; his mission was much bigger than that. So Satan was willing to do everything possible to divert Jesus and the people's attention from his true mission—going to the cross.

For Jesus' third test, Satan promised a shortcut to success. He would give Jesus all the great nations of the world if he would only bow down and worship Satan. In short, Satan offered the world without God. But Jesus would not let anything come between him and his Father. They had their own plan for a kingdom that would bury anything Satan had to offer.

Jesus then commanded Satan to leave him. As soon as Satan was gone, angels joined Jesus in the desert and provided everything he needed.

Jesus answered, "It is written in the Scriptures, 'A person does not live by eating only bread, but by everything God says.'"

MATTHEW 4:4

Reflection: God launched his Son's ministry with words that were exactly right. Jesus identified with the people, and God identified with him. The greatest rescue mission ever conceived was taking human form. It began with affirmation from the Father of Jesus, and Satan was unable to stop it or change it one iota. The wise Father God must have been proud of his faithful Son.

Although Satan doesn't tempt us with the same enticements he offered Jesus, we all face desert temptations. Will we trust God, or will Satan's deception lead us to go our own way? Will we live according to God's plan or according to our plan? Jesus set the perfect example. He faced Satan with confidence, quoting his Father's trustworthy words.

The LORD says, "You are my witnesses
    and the servant I chose.
I chose you so you would know and believe me,
    so you would understand that I am the true God.
There was no God before me,
    and there will be no God after me.
I myself am the LORD;
    I am the only Savior.
I myself have spoken to you, saved you, and told you these things.
    It was not some foreign god among you.
You are my witnesses, and I am God,"
    says the LORD.
    "I have always been God.
No one can save people from my power;
    when I do something, no one can change it."

ISAIAH 43:10–13

A new birth

At Passover time, Jesus traveled to Jerusalem for the celebration. When he arrived at the temple, he was deeply angered by what he saw. Vendors had turned the temple into a marketplace. They had cattle and sheep conveniently tied up, ready to sell at auction. The noise of marketers had overpowered the real purpose of the temple. Calm had been replaced by chaos.

Jesus was not going to stand by and let his Father's house be turned into a cattle auction. He made a whip and began chasing the vendors and their animals out of the temple. The Jewish leaders demanded to know who gave him the right to disrupt their temple practices, but Jesus refused to let them control his actions.

However, some of the leaders were drawn to this young man who acted with such authority. At night one of these leaders, a man named Nicodemus, came to see Jesus. He was curious about Jesus and his teaching, but what he learned was perplexing and disturbing. Jesus explained that God's kingdom wasn't bound by territorial borders or political allegiances, like Herod's or Caesar's. God's kingdom is spiritual. Citizenship in God's kingdom isn't based on who you are or where you live or what you do; it's based on spiritual birth. To enter the kingdom, a person has to be born again — born of the spirit.

Jesus came to open the doors of heaven and introduce God's people to the world of the spirit. He came to introduce eternal life to a death-bound world. He came to transform a struggling people into spiritually alive people who have God living within them. This was unexpected teaching and difficult for the people to accept. To Nicodemus, Jesus must have seemed a strange mixture of wonder and wisdom.

Reflection: The whole world of religion was about to be turned inside out. This new birth Jesus talked of would move the presence of God from the temple into the hearts of the people. The God of life would now live within his creation. And life would be forever changed. It must have been hard for the people to understand what Jesus was talking about, before experiencing it. It's still hard to understand, unless we've experienced spiritual rebirth.

"God loved the world so much that he gave his one and only Son so that whoever believes in him may not be lost, but have eternal life. God did not send his Son into the world to judge the world guilty, but to save the world through him."

JOHN 3:16–17

147

Shaping his ministry

Jesus began his ministry teaching in synagogues, and very quickly his reputation as a teacher grew. On one occasion during his visit to the local synagogue in Nazareth, the leaders chose him to teach. The room must have been filled with childhood friends, neighbors, and relatives. Jesus read a passage written by Isaiah, predicting God's rescue of his struggling people. Then Jesus astonished everyone by claiming these predictions were coming true as he spoke them.

It was Jesus' mission to put a face on the love of his Father. Therefore his ministry focused on those who felt unloved and alone. He did what Isaiah predicted he would do—encourage the poor, release the imprisoned, and open the eyes of the blind. The God who had always been out of reach was now in their midst, face to face.

The people weren't accustomed to anyone speaking like a prophet, especially a hometown boy. They certainly weren't looking for the son of a carpenter to be standing in their synagogue as the Son of God. They didn't understand his words, and they weren't ready to accept who he was, so in the heat of anger they took him to the edge of a cliff, ready to kill him, but Jesus escaped unharmed. As far as we know, he never returned to Nazareth.

Reflection: Jesus turned a new page in the synagogue that day. The Isaiah reading was the same, but he didn't reflect on its historical setting or interpret its meaning for the future. He announced its fulfillment that day. The plan was to touch ordinary people where they lived—at the point of their need—to lift them out of life's shadows forever. Jesus invested his ministry in giving hope to the hopeless and love to the unloved. And he expects his followers to do the same.

The book of Isaiah the prophet was given to him. He opened the book and found the place where this is written:

"The Lord has put his Spirit in
    me,
  because he appointed me to tell
    the Good News to the poor.
He has sent me to tell the captives
    they are free
  and to tell the blind that they
    can see again.
God sent me to free those who
    have been treated unfairly
  and to announce the time when
    the Lord will show his kind-
    ness."

Jesus closed the book, gave it back to the assistant, and sat down. Everyone in the synagogue was watching Jesus closely. He began to say to them, "While you heard these words just now, they were coming true!"

LUKE 4:17–21

149

Choosing his apostles

Jesus took his message to the people. He traveled from town to town, teaching, healing, and attracting crowds of followers and numbers of opponents. Within months of launching his ministry, an inner circle of followers began to form, and eventually twelve of these followers were chosen to be apostles, men with a special assignment.

After spending all night praying in the mountains, Jesus named those men who were to become his core followers. During his ministry on earth they were never far from his side. They were ordinary men from ordinary places, but with Jesus they became extraordinary. Following Jesus filled their days with surprises. He gave sight to the blind, opened the ears of the deaf, fed people by the thousands, cast out demons, calmed storms, spent entire nights praying, and taught lessons that haunted them for life. As the apostles watched, this amazing man reached into the hearts of people and continually taught them more about the Father.

Even though Peter, James, and John enjoyed an especially close relationship with Jesus, they, too, struggled to know who he was. It was difficult to fit their own vision of the Messiah with their growing knowledge of Jesus. They knew he was a challenging teacher, a compassionate healer, and a powerful prophet, but he didn't seem like a conquering king or a mighty warrior. As close as they were, they didn't immediately accept him as Messiah. They may have walked the dusty roads between Galilee and Jerusalem for months not fully realizing they were eating and drinking with the Son of God.

Reflection: Jesus chose the apostles for a task. They were to know Jesus—his teachings, his mission, his essence—well enough to help others know him, even after he was gone. Jesus is still calling people to that task. He still wants us to know him so we can know the Father and so we can help others meet him. Like the apostles, we must also spend time with Jesus so we can grow beyond our limited visions and expectations.

I loved you as the Father loved me. Now remain in my love. I have obeyed my Father's commands, and I remain in his love. In the same way, if you obey my commands, you will remain in my love. I have told you these things so that you can have the same joy I have and so that your joy will be the fullest possible joy.

This is my command: Love each other as I have loved you. The greatest love a person can show is to die for his friends. You are my friends if you do what I command you. I no longer call you servants, because a servant does not know what his master is doing. But I call you friends, because I have made known to you everything I heard from my Father. You did not choose me; I chose you. And I gave you this work: to go and produce fruit, fruit that will last. Then the Father will give you anything you ask for in my name. This is my command: Love each other.

JOHN 15:9–17

Healing with a message

It didn't take long for Jesus to develop the reputation of a compassionate healer. He healed all parts of the body—eyes, ears, hands, legs, hearts, and souls. Yet sin was the problem he most wanted to heal. And as he grew more popular with the people, the religious leaders grew more threatened.

During one visit to Jerusalem, Jesus walked by a man who had been born blind. Jesus' followers seemed more interested in who was to blame for his condition—who sinned here, he or his parents?—than what could be done for him.

Jesus stopped, made a paste of the dirt at his feet, and rubbed it on the man's eyes. Then he told the man to go wash in the Pool of Siloam. Without questioning, the blind man groped his way to the pool. There he washed the mud from his eyes, and for the first time in his life he could see. He was euphoric about his newly acquired vision of the world, and those who knew him were amazed. But some refused to accept the healing.

While the healed man was still celebrating his sight, soaking in shapes and colors and wonders, the people brought him to the Jewish leaders so he could tell them his story. They were more concerned about whether Jesus should have healed on the Sabbath than about the miraculous healing.

The leaders refused to believe Jesus could have done this, so they called the man's parents to check out the story. His parents confirmed that he was their son and that he had been blind since birth. But they had no idea how he had received his sight. "He's an adult," they responded. "Why don't you ask him?"

The healed man knew only one thing—he could see, whether anybody else accepted it or not. And no one could stop him from believing in the gentle healer who had made it possible.

Reflection: Jesus was the gentle healer, and no condition was too severe or too difficult for his touch. As he gave sight to the blind, opened the ears of the deaf, and cleansed the skin of lepers, he taught spiritual truths. He touched those who were born without sight and those who refused to see.

God is still in the healing business; he is still giving sight to the blind. Instead of being threatened by these events, judging circumstances and questioning validity, may we, like the blind man, celebrate and give God the glory.

Jesus then said, "I came into the world to bring everything into the clear light of day, making all the distinctions clear, so that those who have never seen will see, and those who have made a great pretense of seeing will be exposed as blind."

JOHN 9:39, THE MESSAGE

Jesus the shepherd

It was common to see shepherds leading their sheep on the hillsides around Jerusalem. So with the Jewish leaders and a crowd of people listening, Jesus described himself as the good shepherd. The image communicated instantly.

A good shepherd lived with his sheep. He was constantly concerned for the well-being of his flock and always searching for safe pasture and adequate water. Because of his constant care for them, each sheep recognized its shepherd's voice, and each shepherd knew his sheep by name. When it came time to move from one place to another, the shepherd would lead his helpless sheep, walking ahead of them, never driving them.

Jesus taught his followers that he was a shepherd—the good shepherd—one who sacrifices himself for the sheep he loves. He confessed that he knows who his sheep are. In turn, they know him—and follow him. He sees to it that nothing harms them and that they have everything they need for life. Jesus' sheep, his followers, believe in him and have eternal life, but those who refuse to believe in him don't have eternal life.

Again, some people were threatened by Jesus' claims, and they plotted against him. Some tried to take him and stone him right then, but he escaped because his time to die had not yet come.

Reflection: By calling himself the good shepherd, Jesus helps us visualize the Father's offer to us. Jesus offers a "first name" relationship between himself and each of his followers, and nothing can threaten that relationship. He is the source of our protection and our direction. His love is unquestionable; his presence is perpetual.

His sheep have nothing to fear.

"I am the good shepherd. The good shepherd gives his life for the sheep.... I know my sheep, as the Father knows me. And my sheep know me, as I know the Father. I give my life for the sheep.

"My sheep listen to my voice; I know them, and they follow me. I give them eternal life, and they will never die, and no one can steal them out of my hand. My Father gave my sheep to me. He is greater than all, and no person can steal my sheep out of my Father's hand."

JOHN 10:11–15, 27–29

Teaching the basics

Jesus had an irresistible way with the common people. His words were penetrating and inviting. He knew how to get under the surface straight to the soul. As he talked to people, he would guide the conversation into a spiritual discussion. During one of those discussions, a Jewish scholar asked Jesus what he would have to do to get eternal life.

Jesus asked him what the law taught, and the scholar quoted passages about loving God and loving our neighbor. Then he asked who Jesus considered to be his neighbor. Without introduction Jesus launched into a thought-provoking parable.

One day while a man was traveling between Jerusalem and Jericho, he was attacked by robbers, beaten, and left half-dead on the road. Not long after the attack, a Jewish priest came by, but he didn't stop to help or even speak to the poor man. After the priest, another religious man showed up — and walked by on the other side of the road. No doubt the beaten man would have died that day if it hadn't been for the next traveler, a Samaritan man. Under normal circumstances Jews didn't speak to Samaritans, but this Samaritan had compassion on the Jew, treated his injuries, took him to an inn, and paid the bill until the man had recovered.

Jesus asked the scholar which of the three men was a neighbor to the injured man. The answer was clear: "The one who helped him."

"Then do the same," Jesus replied.

One of the major themes of Jesus' teaching was the art of living as neighbors. He taught formally about kindness and compassion and fairness.

Informally he told stories that explained how to live as neighbors. And although an itinerant, he served as a neighbor to those he met. Along the way he even talked about how to respond when people don't treat us as neighbors.

Reflection: The Samaritan wasn't into rules or keeping score. He didn't talk about his theology or join a discussion of ethics; he simply acted instinctively. He did what needed to be done. That's love—love *does*.

Jesus said…

You're blessed when you're at the end of your rope. With less of you there is more of God and his rule.

You're blessed when you feel you've lost what is most dear to you. Only then can you be embraced by the One most dear to you.

You're blessed when you are content with just who you are—no more, no less. That's the moment you find yourselves proud owners of everything that can't be bought.

You're blessed when you've worked up a good appetite for God. He's food and drink in the best meal you'll ever eat.

You're blessed when you care. At the moment of being 'care-full,' you find yourselves cared for.

You're blessed when you get your inside world—your mind and heart—put right. Then you can see God in the outside world.

You're blessed when you can show people how to cooperate instead of compete or fight. That's when you discover who you really are, and your place in God's family.

You're blessed when your commitment to God provokes persecution. The persecution drives you even deeper into God's kingdom.

Not only that—count yourselves blessed every time people put you down or throw you out or speak lies about you to discredit me. What it means is that the truth is too close for comfort and they are uncomfortable.

MATTHEW 5:3–11, THE
MESSAGE

Telling a story of joy

While the Jewish leaders struggled with Jesus' growing influence, Jesus continued telling his pointed parables. With a crowd gathered around him, Jesus taught that the angels in heaven celebrate when a sinner repents. In fact, the whole reason Jesus came to earth was to save sinners—to welcome those who repent. Then he told this story, which reveals the forgiving love of the holy God.

A man had two sons. When the younger of the two asked for his inheritance so he could leave and do whatever he wanted, the father obliged. So the younger son left home with all his possessions, including some he didn't know he had—his conscience, his memories, his identity.

He found his new freedom intoxicating and tantalizing. But after his money was gone and his friends had deserted him, he was forced to rethink who he was and what he had become. He discovered within his battered self a persistent hunger for home. He'd been so stupid and oh so wrong. His father's servants had a better life than he did. He wanted to go home. So, filled with sorrow and hope he began the journey back.

When his father saw him in the distance, the father ran to him, overjoyed that his son had returned. The son's remorse was swallowed up in the father's forgiveness and in his restoration to the family.

Every Jew who heard this story could identify with it. After all, it was the story of prodigal Israel. In a way, Jesus came to lead them home, to show them the outstretched arms of a loving, forgiving Father who longed to welcome them back.

Reflection: Jesus wanted the people to know the God he called Father. So everything he did and said was designed to throw open the doors of heaven, to grant access to the loving arms of his Father. All we have to do is believe and repent—to trust Jesus' words, to turn from our own stubbornness, and do what it takes to come home. Our part of this homecoming isn't hard. God has made it possible, so why do we wait so long? Why is it so difficult for some of us?

"My Father has given me all things. No one knows the Son, except the Father. And no one knows the Father, except the Son and those whom the Son chooses to tell.

"Come to me, all of you who are tired and have heavy loads, and I will give you rest. Accept my teachings and learn from me, because I am gentle and humble in spirit, and you will find rest for your lives. The teaching that I ask you to accept is easy; the load I give you to carry is light."

MATTHEW 11:27–30

159

Crying for the people

During his last respite from the rising tension in Jerusalem, Jesus received word that his friend Lazarus had died. Against the advice of his followers, Jesus and his followers set out for Bethany, the home of Lazarus and his sisters. Jesus' followers had no idea what an incredible experience it would be.

By the time they arrived, Lazarus had been in the tomb four days. Grief-stricken, his sisters, Mary and Martha, wondered why Jesus hadn't come in time to heal Lazarus. Moved by their tears and the tears of the other mourners, Jesus, the son of God, cried too.

When Jesus got to the tomb, he asked that the stone covering the entrance be moved. He looked up to heaven, praying to his Father, and then called for Lazarus to come out of the tomb. To the amazement of everyone, Lazarus came to life and appeared in front of them all, still wrapped in his graveclothes. Jesus had given him new life, and many people believed in Jesus as the Messiah—the Christ. But when the Jewish leaders heard, they renewed their plans to kill Jesus.

Some time later Jesus came to Bethany again to visit Lazarus and his sisters. As he left Bethany, Jesus headed toward Jerusalem. As he neared the city, he was again overcome with tears. This time a whole city was entombed, and even more tragic than Lazarus's death, they would die because of their hardened hearts, because they refused to hear the voice of

God, because they wouldn't let God save them. No wonder God cried.

Reflection: Nothing was beyond Jesus' reach. He had the power to raise Lazarus from the dead, but still Jesus cried. He cried for those who refused to believe in him. The tears revealed his heart. They show us not only a Father who rejoices when we return to him, but also a Father who feels pain, a God who identifies with human struggles and cries for his people.

Our God is a God of comfort. He knows our grief and understands our pain. Our tears are reminders of his care and comfort.

As Jesus came near Jerusalem, he saw the city and cried for it, saying, "I wish you knew today what would bring you peace. But now it is hidden from you. The time is coming when your enemies will build a wall around you and will hold you in on all sides. They will destroy you and all your people, and not one stone will be left on another. All this will happen because you did not recognize the time when God came to save you."

Luke 19:41–44

Priority on prayer

In the midst of all the confusion, the dishonesty, and mockery surrounding Jesus' last days, Jesus was the model of strength—focused, dignified, and humble. His last night with his apostles began with a dramatic twist. Jesus washed the feet of the apostles—the leader became the servant. Passover was shared. Jesus revealed Judas as the betrayer. And the Lord's Supper was introduced as a memorial to Jesus' death and resurrection. After the meal, Jesus spoke of the Holy Spirit who would come after him to help them; he called them friends and prayed for them.

Then as the group walked toward the Mount of Olives, Jesus took Peter, James, and John into Gethsemane, to the place he'd visited many times before. There He prayed, and they slept. The battle between good and evil raged that night. While Jesus fought the battle in his heart, he talked intimately with his Father, and an angel came to encourage him. Jesus knew what had to be done—he just wished there was another way.

Prayer was always a central part of Jesus' life. After he was baptized, he prayed. After teaching the crowds, he retreated to the hills to pray. Before calling his apostles, he spent all night praying. In preparation for conversations with his apostles, he prayed. He prayed before teaching his apostles how to pray. Just before he raised Lazarus from the dead, he prayed aloud. And in the seclusion of the garden, he prayed. He wasn't asking for a change of plans; he was asking for the feelings of his heart to match the determination of his head. And God granted that request.

Reflection: Prayer is not a ritual or a rite or simply reading the current prayer list. It's personal communication heart to heart with God. It's conversation about life: Father, what do you think about...I'm upset about...I feel trapped; help me find some way out...I'm feeling left out...I'm getting too busy; what can I do to slow down...I'm sorry—I messed up...Thanks for the help. Why are people that way...Tell me what I should do different...I'm really discouraged...Please help my kids get to know you...This is going to be a tough week...The battle is raging in my heart; I need courage to do what I know needs to be done...There's this person I want to meet you...Thanks for getting my attention...Show me the way; I'm lost...

Conversation with the Father is essential for knowing him and staying close to him. Jesus is a model of that.

Jesus said to them, "When you pray, say:

'Father, may your name always be kept holy.
May your kingdom come.
Give us the food we need for each day.
Forgive us for our sins,
    because we forgive everyone who
        has done wrong to us.
And do not cause us to be tempted.'"

Then Jesus said to them, "Suppose one of you went to your friend's house at midnight and said to him, 'Friend, loan me three loaves of bread. A friend of mine has come into town to visit me, but I have nothing for him to eat.' Your friend inside the house answers, 'Don't bother me! The door is already locked, and my children and I are in bed. I cannot get up and give you anything.' I tell you, if friendship is not enough to make him get up to give you the bread, your boldness will make him get up and give you whatever you need. So I tell you, ask, and God will give to you. Search, and you will find. Knock, and the door will open for you. Yes, everyone who asks will receive. The one who searches will find. And everyone who knocks will have the door opened. If your children ask for a fish, which of you would give them a snake instead? Or, if your children ask for an egg, would you give them a scorpion? Even though you are bad, you know how to give good things to your children. How much more your heavenly Father will give the Holy Spirit to those who ask him!"

Luke 11:2–13

The ultimate sacrifice for sin

The darkest day in human history was the day the creation killed the creator. God had purposefully sent his Son as a sacrifice for the sins of all humanity. Blinded to God's reality and threatened by the existence of Jesus, religious leaders trumped up a charge, convicted Jesus, and arranged for his crucifixion. But everything was going as God had planned. He was about to turn an apparent defeat into an eternal victory. He was about to transform an ordinary Friday into a legendary one.

The crucifixion of Jesus was like no other in history, for the pain of those hours was immeasurably more than physical anguish. Certainly he suffered physical pain; he was flogged and scourged, forced to drag his own cross through the streets, and nailed to it, where he hung for excruciating hours. However, while hanging there between heaven and earth, he reached into eternity and grabbed hold of everything that could separate humankind from the Father and took it with him into death. He intentionally accepted the punishment for sin, even though he was sinless. The glorious mystery is that for a time the holy became unholy, perfection bore the weight of the sins of the world.

On the cross Jesus connected with corruption, greed, arrogance, indifference, defiance, sarcasm, obscenity, perversion, abusiveness, callousness, ingratitude, hatred, unfaithfulness, deceitfulness, bitterness, resentment, impatience, hypocrisy, divisiveness, vulgarity, bigotry, self-centeredness, and apathy. In essence Jesus suffered death for millions.

While absorbing the sins of the world, he asked God to forgive those who were crucifying him because they didn't know what they were doing. And in what must have been the deepest agony of all, he cried out for his Father's presence.

Finally it was time. As an unfriendly crowd polluted the air with insults and ridicule, the sky grew dark, and a holy eeriness surrounded the crucifixion scene. It was finished. When Jesus spoke his last words, the earth responded with a rock-splitting, grave-opening earthquake. And the holy veil, the cloth wall covering the entrance to the holiest place of the temple, which symbolized God's presence, was torn from top to bottom. Now the holy God was approachable by everyone, not just the high priest.

Jesus didn't die as a victim but as a glorious victor, and God wasn't done yet.

Reflection: We've heard it before—Jesus paid the debt for our sins. He paid it all. But that news is hard to grasp. We hope God has forgotten the guilt of our sins. We hope Jesus took our guilt with him when he died. But

At one time you were separated from God. You were his enemies in your minds, and the evil things you did were against God. But now God has made you his friends again. He did this through Christ's death in the body so that he might bring you into God's presence as people who are holy, with no wrong, and with nothing of which God can judge you guilty.

COLOSSIANS 1:21–22

we're not sure. Satan failed to stop Jesus, so now his attention is turned full force on God's people, and our doubt is a measure of his success.

It's past time to believe, fully believe in Jesus' sacrifice and in God's gift. The only thing in this world that can limit his grace is our lack of faith.

Then Jesus called the crowd to him, along with his followers. He said, "If people want to follow me, they must give up the things they want. They must be willing even to give up their lives to follow me. Those who want to save their lives will give up true life. But those who give up their lives for me and for the Good News will have true life. It is worth nothing for them to have the whole world if they lose their souls. They could never pay enough to buy back their souls. The people who live now are living in a sinful and evil time. If people are ashamed of me and my teaching, the Son of Man will be ashamed of them when he comes with his Father's glory and with the holy angels."

MARK 8:34–38

Resurrection victory

As evening came that Friday, Jesus' body was removed from the cross, and with the help of Nicodemus, Joseph of Arimathea prepared it for burial and placed it in his own tomb. The apostles had scattered, and a few loyal friends mourned.

No doubt Satan rejoiced and claimed victory. He had the Son of God locked up in death. His empire must have resounded with triumphant shouts. Truth is, however, when Jesus died, Satan lost all control over him. Jesus was and forever would be in the hands of the author of resurrection.

In the confusion and pain of loss everyone appeared to have forgotten Jesus' promise to return. Then, in the stillness of Sunday's dawn, the almighty God of life, the eternal Father broke the bonds of death and gave new life to his Son's lifeless body. By the end of the day, not only had the news of an empty tomb spread throughout the city, but the risen Jesus had been seen at least five different times.

After his resurrection, for the first time Jesus called the apostles his "brothers" and referred to his Father as their Father. They were now part of the family. The holy, transcendent, sovereign God turned his Son's resurrection into an open invitation to a new life and a new relationship with him and each other. Even death proved impotent against the all-powerful God.

Reflection: The great war between God and Satan, light and dark, good and evil has been won. Jesus, the Son of God, descended into Satan's domain and returned. Although the daily battles with evil remain, our faith in Jesus' sacrifice for us and our confidence in his resurrection have rendered the fear of death powerless. After all, God is our Father, and Jesus is our brother.

"People of Israel, listen to these words: Jesus from Nazareth was a very special man. God clearly showed this to you by the miracles, wonders, and signs he did through Jesus. You all know this, because it happened right here among you. Jesus was given to you, and with the help of those who don't know the law, you put him to death by nailing him to a cross. But this was God's plan which he had made long ago; he knew all this would happen. God raised Jesus from the dead and set him free from the pain of death, because death could not hold him.

"Jesus was lifted up to heaven and is now at God's right side."

ACTS 2:22–24, 33

Waiting for God

For forty days the resurrected Jesus walked again among his followers, teaching them and preparing them for the exciting days ahead. The Jewish leaders were baffled; despite their frantic investigations they couldn't find Jesus' body nor successfully debunk his resurrection. Even the apostles, despite seeing the risen Jesus, had trouble believing what they had seen. But following Jesus' request, they traveled north to the Sea of Galilee, to the area where it all began for them.

There Jesus helped them understand all that had happened. He strengthened their faith and encouraged their hearts. This teacher they had lived with, listened to, and wondered about, this man who had washed their feet, accepted their failures, and transformed their lives, was now the risen King. Everything, including the crucifixion, had happened exactly as God had planned. Jesus was now the ultimate authority in heaven and on earth, and he had a new assignment for his apostles. These handpicked, unimpressive men were charged with telling the story of Jesus to anyone who would listen. They were to share what they had seen and heard and experienced while Jesus was on the earth.

Back in Jerusalem, Jesus urged them to wait for God's power and his plan for the future. He would transform them into powerful witnesses far beyond their limited abilities. Jesus blessed them, then ascended into heaven. Two angels appeared telling the followers not to focus on Jesus' leaving, because one day he would come back, just as he left. So the apostles waited for God's power.

Reflection: The risen Jesus thrilled the hearts of his followers, especially the apostles. Every moment with him was cherished, but he left them with questions still unanswered. They weren't even sure what was next. They merely knew they were to wait. Every day must have been filled with anticipation and wonder. They had no access to the master plan. They were uncertain of what they were waiting for, but in faith they waited.

They were waiting for God to do what they could not do—to transform them, to fill them with his Spirit. Often our task is the same—to wait for him to do his work in us.

Jesus led his followers as far as Bethany, and he raised his hands and blessed them. While he was blessing them, he was separated from them and carried into heaven. They worshiped him and returned to Jerusalem very happy. They stayed in the Temple all the time, praising God.

LUKE 24:50–53

The birth of the church

Within days, it was time to celebrate Pentecost, the Jewish day of thanksgiving. Jews from all over the known world gathered in Jerusalem. Suddenly the sound of a powerful wind filled the house where Jesus' followers were meeting. The waiting was over. God's power had come. They were filled with the Holy Spirit, and people were both amazed and confused.

Strange things were happening—people speaking languages without training, the sound of wind without wind, and fire without burning. Jesus' followers lost themselves in praise. Very likely they could hear his voice in the wind and could feel his presence in the fire.

But when bystanders accused them of being drunk, Peter stood in defense of the believers. He was not schooled in theology or public speaking. Before he met Jesus, he had been an anonymous fisherman on the Sea of Galilee. He knew the language of a fisherman, not that of a teacher.

He was an unlikely candidate in many ways. He was the man who jumped out of the boat and walked on water, then had to be rescued by Jesus when fear set in. He was the first to proclaim Jesus as the Son of God, but when Jesus was arrested, Peter denied even knowing him. He had been to the mountaintop and in the garden with Jesus. It was this man of mixed mind who stood and boldly preached the first sermon about Jesus. It wasn't long. It was direct and to the point—God sent Jesus, you rejected him, you killed him, God raised him, you're guilty, but God will forgive, and you can receive his Holy Spirit. Three thousand responded that day, and God's church was born.

The Holy Spirit began his work by transforming this untrained, unsophisticated unknown into a charismatic, passionate leader in the formation of God's church. The uneducated fisherman from Galilee became a powerful, persuasive preacher. The Spirit was, and is, exactly what God's people needed. Under his direction they shared new life together. They ate together and prayed together and praised together and welcomed new believers together.

Reflection: God's Holy Spirit helped the apostles understand and recall Jesus' time with them. In that holy Pentecost moment their vision of life was changed. The dream of overthrowing Roman occupation, of restoring the nation to Israel's control vanished. They gave up their dreams, their fears, and eventually their lives for the sake of Jesus. With God's Holy Spirit these Galileans were transformed, and they were ready to tell the story of Jesus—to introduce the "good news."

The Holy Spirit changes everything. But strange as it may seem, many of us resist his power. We fear what we cannot control. We

"But I tell you the truth, it is better for you that I go away. When I go away, I will send the Helper to you. If I do not go away, the Helper will not come. When the Helper comes, he will prove to the people of the world the truth about sin, about being right with God, and about judgment. He will prove to them that sin is not believing in me. He will prove to them that being right with God comes from my going to the Father and not being seen anymore."

JOHN 16:7–10

are uncomfortable with the unknown. We struggle with seeking help outside ourselves and end up watching from a distance, missing God's power and growing more miserable and fearful.

Oh how we need a fresh awakening to the Spirit's presence and power.

"No one has ever seen this,
    and no one has ever heard about it.
No one has ever imagined
    what God has prepared for those
    who love him."
But God has shown us these things through the Spirit.

The Spirit searches out all things, even the deep secrets of God. Who knows the thoughts that another person has? Only a person's spirit that lives within him knows his thoughts. It is the same with God. No one knows the thoughts of God except the Spirit of God. Now we did not receive the spirit of the world, but we received the Spirit that is from God so that we can know all that God has given us. And we speak about these things, not with words taught us by human wisdom but with words taught us by the Spirit.

1 CORINTHIANS 2:9–13

Peter shares good news

God's young church was filled with encouragement. The apostles healed people as Jesus had done. The believers ate together, worked together, and praised God together, and more were joining their numbers every day. As they grew, they expanded from Jerusalem to Samaria and into Judea.

After teaching in small churches surrounding Jerusalem, Peter settled for a while in the port city of Joppa. There God prepared his heart to introduce Jesus to Gentiles, the non-Jewish people. Until now all the believers were Jews. The Spirit led Peter to a Roman centurion named Cornelius living in Caesarea. While Peter was telling Cornelius and his friends and family about God's acceptance of anyone who believes in him, the Holy Spirit came on the crowd—as he had done at Pentecost. Peter baptized them and accepted them as brothers. God was opening the door for both Jew and Gentile just as he had promised.

Back in Jerusalem, Peter had to defend his actions, but after he told the story of what had happened, the Jewish Christians could do nothing but praise God and learn to welcome their Gentile brothers into the church family. The promise God had made to Abraham long ago was finally coming true—every nation would be blessed by his descendant.

Reflection: Although it was relatively easy for the Jewish people to accept that God had opened the door of forgiveness and eternal life to Gentiles, it proved difficult to live with. As the church grew and Gentiles were added, one of the greatest challenges was keeping their unity in spite of their differences.

Racial and cultural differences still plague the church. Satan knows how to divide us, and he knows if we are divided, we lose our effectiveness in the world. Our prayers and efforts for unity are powerful weapons in the spiritual battle that continues to rage.

Peter began to speak: "I really understand now that to God every person is the same. In every country God accepts anyone who worships him and does what is right. You know the message that God has sent to the people of Israel is the Good News that peace has come through Jesus Christ. Jesus is the Lord of all people!"

ACTS 10:34–36

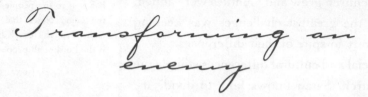

Transforming an enemy

The believers continued to spread the word all the way to Antioch, where God's church grew strong and vibrant. In fact, a few years later when Jerusalem was suffering a famine, the church in Antioch sent relief funds to the Jerusalem church. And the believers were first called Christians in Antioch.

Peter had been a courageous leader for God's church, but now the church needed a traveling missionary who could communicate with the non-Jewish as well as the Jewish culture. God found just the man. Among those Jewish leaders in Jerusalem who were dedicated to snuffing out this growing religious menace known as Christianity was a young man named Saul. He had a unique background as a Jewish scholar and a Roman citizen, and he was dedicated to destroying God's new church.

On his way to shut down the churches in Damascus, Saul was knocked to the ground by a blinding flash of light. Jesus—the light of the world— was about to make a great apostle out of a vigilant enemy. Jesus called him by name and told him to wait in Damascus to learn what he must do. The rational, confident, persistent, and now humbled Saul had been chosen to serve Jesus, not fight him. After he was baptized and met with the disciples, he headed off to Arabia, perhaps to let this massive transformation sink deep within him.

Three years passed before Saul traveled to Jerusalem to introduce himself as one called by Jesus for a mission. There he spent fifteen days with Peter. What a meeting it must have been. They were so different—Peter, the untrained fisherman, and Paul, the scholar—but they were filled with the same Spirit, and they had been called by the same Lord.

It didn't take long for Saul to be affirmed by the apostles and for him to begin the mission of his life—taking the story of Jesus to the Gentile world. From this time forward, Paul (Saul's Roman name) lived for Jesus. The Spirit of God would do great things through this transformed man, but Saul would also suffer much for Jesus in the process.

Reflection: For Peter, transformation seemed to be filled with ups and down—a process. For Paul, transformation was a glorious act of grace—an event. Both are valid. God is the same, people are different.

God's willingness to love us while we're still far from him and his ability to work with our weaknesses as well as our strengths makes the Christian adventure such an attractive one. But even with all that God has done, turning our lives over to him may be a constant battle.

I thank Christ Jesus our Lord, who gave me strength, because he trusted me and gave me this work of serving him. In the past I spoke against Christ and persecuted him and did all kinds of things to hurt him. But God showed me mercy, because I did not know what I was doing. I did not believe. But the grace of our Lord was fully given to me, and with that grace came the faith and love that are in Christ Jesus.

1 TIMOTHY 1:12–14

179

Churches cover the earth

Paul's first mission tour took him to the province of Galatia. Even though it was Paul's practice to go to the local synagogue first, his teaching attracted crowds of Gentiles, and that angered many local Jews. In Iconium, angry Jews threatened to stone him, and in Lystra, agitators from other towns turned the people against Paul and his fellow missionaries. This time they succeeded in stoning Paul and leaving him for dead, but with God's help he made it to Derbe, where many Gentiles became Christians. Then Paul went back to each town, encouraging the new Christians before he returned to Antioch.

Paul's mission efforts were interrupted by a special conference in Jerusalem. A group of Jerusalem Christians wanted all the non-Jewish Christians to keep the law too. Paul argued against requiring Gentiles to keep Jewish laws. No one was saved by keeping the law—no one. Paul preached that both Jews and Gentiles are saved by faith in the grace of Jesus.

Paul prevailed at the conference and then began his second missionary tour, returning to the Galatian churches. Once he reached Troas, he sailed for Philippi and established churches in Philippi, Thessalonica, Berea, and Athens. Then he broke with his usual pattern and spent eighteen months in Corinth. Many people in this large city became Christians before Paul returned to Antioch and Jerusalem.

Paul's third tour took him to the churches established in his previous trips, but this time he stayed in Ephesus for three years, and a strong church grew there. After about three months in the synagogue Paul moved his work to the school of Tyrannus, a public lecture hall. There he could teach about Jesus every day. During those times, God's Spirit blessed Paul with unusual powers of healing; even Paul's handkerchiefs and pieces of clothing were able to heal the sick and exorcise demons. After some impostors tried to cast out demons in the name of Paul's Jesus, God moved the people to reject the magic and sorcery in their lives. They burned their books and honored Jesus citywide.

In Ephesus, Paul appointed elders for the church and guided them in how to lead God's church without him. The Christians there grew strong in the Lord, becoming a powerful influence for good in a struggling culture.

After spending his life planting churches, Paul finally ended up in Rome where he wrote many of the teaching letters contained in the New Testament.

Reflection: The Holy Spirit filled Paul with courage and fire and a passion for the story of Jesus. He lived for his mission regardless of the consequences. He had learned to let God

Paul sent to Ephesus and called for the elders of the church. When they came to him, he said, "...I don't care about my own life. The most important thing is that I complete my mission, the work that the Lord Jesus gave me—to tell people the Good News about God's grace....

"...Be careful for yourselves and for all the people the Holy Spirit has given to you to care for. You must be like shepherds to the church of God, which he bought with the death of his own son....

"Now I am putting you in the care of God and the message about his grace. It is able to give you strength, and it will give you the blessings God has for all his holy people."

ACTS 20:17–32

181

lead while keeping his eyes open for every opportunity along the way. It was God's will that his church would transform the culture, and that the church leaders would keep the church strong after the apostles were gone.

The church is not a place, but people—people who are light to those around them.

"Listen! I am coming soon! I will bring my reward with me, and I will repay each one of you for what you have done. I am the Alpha and the Omega, the First and the Last, the Beginning and the End.

"Happy are those who wash their robes so that they will receive the right to eat the fruit from the tree of life and may go through the gates into the city."

Jesus, the One who says these things are true, says, "Yes, I am coming soon."

Amen. Come, Lord Jesus!

REVELATION 22:12–14, 20

He's coming again

As the story of Jesus was told from city to city, the Holy Spirit continued to keep the believers united and strong. Most of the apostles, including Paul, were martyred for their faith in Jesus. But while John was still alive on the island of Patmos, God blessed him with a vision for the ages.

In the vision John was granted entrance to the home of God in all its breathtaking, glorious splendor. Here sits the throne of God—the creator; the God of Abraham, Isaac, and Jacob; the I AM God of Moses; the almighty, holy God of heaven and earth; the Father God of Jesus—the center of all power and authority and majesty. His sovereignty is eternal and unrivaled. In his absolute holiness he radiates dazzling light and brilliant color. At the throne everyone gives honor and glory and praise to the God who was and is and is to come. A rainbow encircles the throne like a halo, but a storm brews behind it as though the anger of God is building to an inevitable crescendo of judgment on the earth.

In the vision John saw Jesus—the lamb, the lion, the warrior rider on a white horse—coming back in blazing glory to redeem his faithful believers. John saw him face to face. And he saw the day when everyone, believer and nonbeliever, will see Jesus and bow before him and worship him.

John's vision ends with a blessing to those who heed the words that Jesus is coming again, and when he does, he will take us home with him to heaven, and we will live with him forever. We will discover the presence of God lost in the Garden of Eden.

We will be home.

Reflection: Like Israel of old, God's people await his promised coming. The closer we feel to our great God, the more we anticipate Jesus' return. For the Christian it will be a incredible day of affirmation, when Jesus speaks for us. But for those who have refused the gift of God, for those who have denied Jesus and lived for themselves, it will be a day of reckoning and rejection and agony.

On that day every knee will bow before the holy God of heaven. Let us bow now and long for the coming call to live with him in heaven.

Jesus said, "Don't let your hearts be troubled. Trust in God, and trust in me. There are many rooms in my Father's house; I would not tell you this if it were not true. I am going there to prepare a place for you. After I go and prepare a place for you, I will come back and take you to be with me so that you may be where I am."

JOHN 14:1–3

From John.... Grace and peace to you from the One who is and was and is coming, and from the seven spirits before his throne, and from Jesus Christ. Jesus is the faithful witness, the first among those raised from the dead. He is the ruler of the kings of the earth.

He is the One who loves us, who made us free from our sins with the blood of his death. He made us to be a kingdom of priests who serve God his Father. To Jesus Christ be glory and power forever and ever! Amen.

REVELATION 1:4–6

Are you in the book?

The Bible is the story of God's unstoppable love. It is his Word, filled with his promises, his plans, and his purposes. In its pages God tells the epic redemption story—the reconciliation of humanity. It is *his* diary. Although it's a finished document, the story is unending. The impact of God's intervention in this world, his transforming work in the lives of his people is still being written. Our encounters with God won't be found in the pages of the Bible. We're in another of God's books—the book of life.

Do you realize how vital it is for your name to be in God's book of life? The book of life isn't just a list of people who have lived on earth; it's much more. It's heaven's invitation list—the people who know the King of kings. It's the list of eternal life.

All our lives we struggle to get on someone's list—a dean's list, a guest list, an acceptance list, the A list, a winner's list. At best they're a flash in the pan compared to the list of life in God's book. God's list is an annotated one; it retells the stories of our times with God himself—times when our soul was touched, times when our faith was tested and held firm, moments of closeness when the Spirit of God deepened our relationship with the Father. With our names in his book of life we are God's people.

How do we continue to seek out these moments with God? Where can we find these "diary" times? They will be unique to each of us, but our ancestors in God's diary illustrate important aspects of spending time with God.

LISTENING IN SOLITUDE

Solitude has long been a way to find holy ground. Since the fall, men and women have longed to return to the closeness of the Garden. We long for companionship with God—the intimacy Adam and Eve lost. Jacob wrestled with God in his aloneness and received God's blessing and a new name.

While hiding from his enemy, Gideon was challenged and empowered by God to lead his people to victory over the Midianites. Samuel was alone in his bed when God called him into a life of service. David discovered the heart of God while leading sheep from pasture to pasture. In a cave on Mount Sinai Elijah heard the whisper of God, and his ministry was refocused and his heart reassured. Jesus customarily spent time alone with his Father, and Paul did some of his best work isolated in a prison cell. During moments of solitude they all heard God's voice, and their lives were changed by his presence, for when God touches us, we are never the same.

Following in obedience

When people follow God's lead regardless of the destination, they walk hand in hand with him. Noah followed God's directions, built a boat, and repopulated the earth. Abraham followed God into a friendship and a lifetime of walking the promised land. By staying true to God's leading, Joseph found God's holy presence even in the prisons of Egypt and saved the people from starvation. Daniel's three friends marched into the fire in a demonstration of their faith in God, and God not only protected them, he met them there. When Jesus was in the garden, he committed himself to following God's plan even if it meant being crucified on a cross. The apostle John followed God into exile on the island of Patmos—and into a vision of heaven. In obedience, people of God find a patient, loving Shepherd who leads them into safe and green pastures.

Remaining steady in crisis

A crisis requires resources beyond our supply, obliging us to trust the unseen but all-powerful God. Although Job spent most of his crisis time trying to understand why misfortunes had befallen him, he never cursed God or turned his back on him, and God restored to Job abundantly more than he had lost. At the Red Sea, Moses was confronted with an impossible task—an angry Egyptian army on one side and the sea on the other. But Moses told the people to stand firm and watch God work the impossible. Joshua faced the formidable task of taking the promised land for God, reassured by the leader of God's armies and a series of impressive miracles. Rebuilding the wall of Jerusalem amidst discouragement within and enemies without proved daunting, until God brought Nehemiah to town. Despite beatings, stonings, shipwrecks, imprisonment, and threats, Paul proclaimed the good news in all places at all times, and gave birth to much of our New Testament. In crisis times they all trusted in God's power and found him to be present and dependable.

CONFESSING WEAKNESS AND SIN

From the time of Seth, when humankind started praying, God has heard billions of confessions—each of them personal. From our times of weakness, a greater recognition of and reliance upon God's strength is born. David fell on his face and wept over his sin with Bathsheba, and God forgave his guilt and strengthened him to become one of the most beloved leaders of Israel. Jonah prayed from the depths of the sea, and God forgave and rescued him and used him to bring about a mighty revival in Nineveh. Isaiah confessed his unworthiness, and God purified him and called him to a great ministry. When Ezra read God's Word to the people, they wept over their sins, and Nehemiah told the people to cry no longer but to realize that the joy of the Lord was their strength. In the garden, Jesus confessed his desire for God's will to be fulfilled in another way, but God strengthened him to face the days ahead in order to save mankind. In confession God's people experience his mercy, his compassion, and the healing power of his forgiveness.

REPENTING OF WRONG

God loves it when his people return to him—when they repent. Samuel led the people to destroy their idols and return to God. The prophets Jeremiah

189

and Amos and Micah called for repentance and revival. Josiah tore his clothes and cried, and a new awareness of God—a revival—swept the land. John preached repentance and revival in preparation for the coming Messiah. Jesus told stories of repentance and celebration, but the repentance that rocked the Jewish world was the repentance at Pentecost. The believers were given new life and a new Spirit, and they were welcomed into a new family. They discovered the God who could heal anything. The past was dead, and the future was focused on Jesus and the apostles' teaching. Now their days were spent celebrating their kinship with God.

PRAISING GOD

When people praise God, they may sing or clap their hands or shout or testify to express their appreciation to the God who has forgiven them and saved them and knows them. After the Hebrews were safely delivered from the Egyptians and the Red Sea, the first thing they did was sing praises to God. David and Solomon wrote songs of praise that continue today to inspire praises to God. When the temple was dedicated, the people praised God for days. Jehoshaphat fought and defeated his enemies, led by a choir singing praises to God. When battles were won, the Israelites praised God. When Hezekiah celebrated the Passover, they praised God twice. When Nehemiah finished the wall, the people praised God. When Jesus was born, the angels praised God. When the handicapped man was healed, he jumped in praise. When Jesus was raised, the believers praised God. As people praise him and lift up his name in worship and song, God comes close to his people.

SURRENDERING IN BROKENNESS

We are a stubborn people. We want to do everything ourselves. Even when God fixes something beyond our capabilities, we prefer to think we did it ourselves. Yet God is perhaps most present in our surrender, in our brokenness. He is there to work a miracle—to transform us, to heal us, to raise us back up. He transformed David from a shepherd to a king. He shaped a dynamic preacher and leader out of a frightened fisherman named Peter. Paul, the feared enemy of the early church, changed into a fearless emissary for Jesus and for the very church he had tried to destroy. The apostle John, a son of thunder, became a great spokesman for love. And Jesus' death on the cross opened the very doors of heaven for the world.

Our task is to surrender, to praise, to confess, to repent, to yield in our brokenness, to listen in solitude, to follow in obedience, to remain faithful in crisis. And the God of all love will do the transforming. Without God, we groan with incompleteness, alone in this life. With God comes life and life abundant. With God we begin our journey back to paradise, and the story will end much where it began—with the Creator and the created in perfect harmony and kinship.